SPI
EGE
L&G
RAU

Alice Herz, Prague, circa 1924

To Linda
with gratitude
Caroline Stoessinger

A Century *of* Wisdom

*Lessons from the Life of
Alice Herz-Sommer,
the World's Oldest Living
Holocaust Survivor*

Caroline Stoessinger

SPIEGEL & GRAU   NEW YORK   2012

Published in the United States by Spiegel & Grau,
an imprint of The Random House Publishing Group,
a division of Random House, Inc., New York.

SPIEGEL & GRAU and design is a registered trademark of
Random House, Inc.

Photographs, excluding the frontispiece, are by Yuri Dojc and are
reprinted by permission of the photographer.

Library of Congress Cataloging-in-Publication Data

Stoessinger, Caroline.
A century of wisdom: lessons from the life of Alice Herz-Sommer, the
world's oldest living Holocaust survivor / Caroline Stoessinger.
p. cm.
ISBN 978-0-8129-9281-6
eBook ISBN 978-0-679-64401-9
1. Herz-Sommer, Alice, 1903– 2. Jews—Czech Republic—Prague—
Biography. 3. Women pianists—Biography. 4. Theresienstadt
(Concentration camp). 5. Holocaust survivors—Israel—Biography. 6.
Holocaust survivors—England—London—Biography. 7. Prague (Czech
Republic)—Biography. I. Title.
DS135.C97H488 2012
940.53'18092—dc23   [B] 2011035168

Printed in the United States of America on acid-free paper

www.spiegelandgrau.com

6 8 9 7 5

Book Design by Liz Cosgrove

For Anna

No longer forward nor behind
I look in hope or fear,
But, grateful, take the good I find,
The best of now and here.

—John Greenleaf Whittier, 1859

FOREWORD

Václav Havel

A Century of Wisdom is a deeply moving account of the epic journey of one woman who has crossed decades and national borders to defy death and to inspire us all. Set against both the beauty of our Central European culture and the tragic events of the twentieth century that shut Czechoslovakia off from the rest of the world for nearly fifty years, Alice Herz-Sommer's life illustrates a deep ethical and spiritual strength. Her memories are our memories. Through her suffering we recall our darkest hours. Through her example we rise to find the best in ourselves.

At 108 years old, Alice enjoys telling stories from the lives of great thinkers—from Gustav Mahler to Sigmund Freud and Viktor Frankl, from Martin Buber to Leo Baeck—who have left an indelible impression. With her music—as a concert pianist and as a teacher—she has influenced countless students, their children, and their children's children, just as she comforted her fellow inmates in the Theresienstadt concentration camp with her talents. Since the war, Alice has been equal parts teacher and student; she has spent the balance of her life in untiring pursuit of knowledge and understanding of who we are as humans, as a community, and as individuals.

Alice has said, "I never give up hope." This sentiment resonates strongly with me, for I believe that hope is related to the very feeling that life has meaning, and as long as we feel that it does, we have a reason to live. Alice's irrepressible optimism inspires me. She has survived, I believe, so that the world may know her story, our story, of truth and beauty in the face of evil. Not only can we learn from Alice today but future generations can take wisdom and hope from her richly textured life.

CONTENTS

Contents

PRELUDE

At 108 years old, Alice is the world's oldest Holocaust survivor, as well as the world's oldest concert pianist. An eyewitness to the entire last century and the first decade of this one, she has seen it all—the best and the worst of mankind. She has lived her life against a backdrop of good amid the chaos of evil, yet she continues to throw her head back in laughter with the same optimism she had as a child.

Despite her years of imprisonment in the Theresienstadt concentration camp and the murders of her mother, husband, and friends at the hands of the Nazis, Alice is victorious in her ability to move on and to live each day in the present. She has wasted no time on bitterness toward her oppressors and the executioners of her family. Aware that hatred eats the soul of the hater rather than the hated, Alice reasons, "I am still grateful for life. Life is a present."

A Century of Wisdom tells of one woman's lifelong determination—in the face of some of the worst ills and heartaches—to bring good to the world. In Alice's story we can find lessons for our own twenty-first-century lives. This is Alice's gift to us.

Her name, Herz-Sommer, means "heart of summer," although she was born on a bitterly cold day, November 26, 1903, in Prague. Her parents, Friedrich and Sofie Herz, called her Alice, which means "of the noble kind." Her father was a successful merchant, and her mother was highly educated and moved in circles of well-known artists and writers that included Gustav Mahler, Rainer Maria Rilke, Thomas Mann, Stefan Zweig, and Franz Kafka.

Alice grew up in a secure and peaceful environment, in which reading and concertgoing were the major forms of entertainment; neighbors would help one another in times of sickness; and families could calculate their interest and retirement for many years to come. Before World War II, Alice was well on her way to a distinguished career as a concert pianist. Her mother's profound love and deep knowledge of music as well as her friendship with Mahler provided Alice with inspiration, and she decided to become a pianist at an early age. Alice remembers accompanying her mother by train to Vienna two days before her fourth birthday to hear Mahler conduct the farewell performance of his Second Symphony with the Hofoper Orchestra on November 24, 1907. Alice said that after the concert her mother talked with the composer, and then "I spoke a little bit with Gustav Mahler." Alice tucks in her lips and raises her shoulders in her expression of wonder at that moment in the presence of genius. Most likely Alice was with her mother when Sofie, together with Arnold Schoenberg, stood in the crowd at the railroad station to wave as Mahler's train slowly left Vienna the morning after the concert.

Years later, after auditioning for Artur Schnabel, she was convinced that a career as a pianist was within her reach. Frequently she was the featured piano soloist with the Czech Philharmonic, and she completed a number of commercial recordings, receiving glowing reviews in *Prager Tagblatt,* the German paper in Prague, from Max Brod, Kafka's friend and biographer.

But the world around Alice had gone mad. Czech laws were abolished. The city was deluged with Nazi flags. Alice snapped a photograph of her three-year-old child standing in front of a sign that read JUDEN EINTRITT VERBOTEN (Jews are forbidden to enter) and barred his entrance from his favorite park. After the Anschluss, in March 1938, Alice's sisters and their families began making frantic preparations to immigrate to Palestine; Alice and her husband chose to stay behind with their young son to care for her aging mother, who would be one of the first to be sent to Theresienstadt. Instinctively Alice understood that she would never see her mother again as she watched her trudge with her heavy rucksack into an enormous building the Nazis had confiscated to use for a human collection center. "Where they burn books, they will ultimately burn people also," Heinrich Heine had cautioned a century earlier. Still, most people did not believe the dire predictions.

By early 1939, remnants of Czechoslovakia's army and government, along with the country's president, Edvard Beneš, had fled to England, where trainloads of children wearing name tags had been shipped to live with strangers. All doors to the democratic world were slamming shut. The British Embassy was closing, and the Americans, too, would be leaving. Nazi soldiers equipped with machine guns patrolled the streets. The last train headed for London, packed with more than three hundred Jewish children, never left the station; most of those children disappeared forever.

In July 1943, Alice and her husband, the businessman and amateur violinist Leopold Sommer, and their six-year-old son, Raphaël, or "Rafi," were notified that they too were being deported to Theresienstadt. Alice had hoped she would find her mother there, but Sofie had already been sent on farther east, most likely to Treblinka.

Theresienstadt was no ordinary concentration camp. From the outside it looked like a very crowded small city where thousands rushed around and music often could be heard: it was Hitler's propaganda machine at work. The Führer had touted Theresienstadt as the place where distinguished Jewish musicians, writers, artists, and the elderly would be protected from the war. The truth was that the camp was a heavily guarded ghetto, a transit station to Auschwitz and other Nazi killing fields throughout eastern Europe. Inside the walls, the gifted and the intelligentsia from Czechoslovakia, Austria, Holland, Denmark, and Germany suffered from constant hunger, cold, infectious diseases, torture, and death. Of the 156,000 Jews imprisoned in Theresienstadt, a mere 17,500 would survive. Between 1942 and 1945, more than 15,000 Jewish children were rounded up and shipped to Theresienstadt. Approximately 100 survived, among them Rafi.

Nevertheless, unlike in the other camps, there was a patina of normal life in Theresienstadt. Despite the terror and deprivation, musicians practiced, actors performed, professors gave lectures, artists drew on scraps of paper, and friends even exchanged jokes. Eventually the Nazis ordered performances for propaganda purposes. What they did not realize was that these concerts would help both listeners and performers to survive.

And so it was for Alice Herz-Sommer, who played more than one hundred programs for her fellow inmates and secretly managed to give piano lessons to children in the camp.

. . .

When the Soviet Army liberated Theresienstadt, on May 8, 1945, Alice and Rafi returned to Prague only to discover strangers living in their apartment. Having few resources and finding almost no one from her past, Alice made the decision in 1949 to immigrate to Israel, where she would reunite with her sisters and their families as well as with friends, including Max Brod. She went on to form a new life, and at forty-five years of age, Alice learned Hebrew. She supported herself and Rafi by teaching at the Conservatory of the Jerusalem Academy of Music (later renamed the Rubin Academy of Music), but although she continued to perform in Israel and later, infrequently, in Europe, Alice never revived her international career. The lost years in the concentration camp combined with her need to earn money and to care for her son consumed her time and energy.

Rafi grew up to be a successful cellist, and at eighty-three years old, Alice traded countries once again, immigrating to London to be near her son. Her greatest heartbreak came a few years later, with his sudden death at the age of sixty-five.

I first met Alice in her home in London when I began working on a documentary film about her life. For years I had been absorbed in music of the Holocaust and particularly music in the Theresienstadt Ghetto, where my husband had lost his grandparents. How could anyone play concerts or write music under such conditions? I had heard about Alice from other Theresienstadt survivors and from long talks with Joža Karas, a Czech émigré musician who had conducted many hours of taped interviews with Alice in the 1970s.

In response to the 9/11 tragedy, Alice said to me, "Of course it was terrible, but why are you so shocked? Good and evil have been around since prehistoric times. It is how we handle it, how we respond, that is important." Alice laughed—disconcerting as it was to me in that moment, I would soon discover that particular laugh was her way of emphasizing the importance of her words. Gently scolding me she continued, "Isn't this wonderful? You took a plane and came to London in only a few hours. We can sit together and talk. We are alive. We have music. You are rich like me because you are a pianist. No one can ever destroy this fortune." Then she reminded me of something Leonard Bernstein said after the assassination of President John F. Kennedy. "This is our answer to violence, we will make music more beautifully, urgently, and more passionately than ever before."

Even though she has not performed publicly for the past quarter of a century, Alice remains true to her commitment, practicing Bach and Beethoven, Chopin and Schubert—all from memory—at least three hours daily. She frequently plays chamber music in her home in the evenings with professionals who stop by to visit her. Alice switches languages easily and fluently. While German was her first language and Czech her second, she is articulate in English, French, and Hebrew.

Alice lives alone, but she is not lonely. She has everything and nothing—everything spiritual, but nothing material. The bank account of her mind is priceless. Her material possessions include only very old clothes, an antique television and well-used video player, a few photographs, and her indispensable upright piano.

While her face is lined and marred with age spots from years in the Jerusalem sun, Alice's smile is her most noticeable physical characteristic. Generated from somewhere inside her, it radiates and explodes into warm and welcoming mirth. Alice's laughter is at once inquisitive and nonjudgmental. It reflects a world of memories colored with the love that comes from her years of understanding.

She exercises daily by taking long walks, moving slowly and cautiously in sneakers to avoid falls; she shuns both a walker and a hearing aid. Until recently Alice was studying history and philosophy at the University of the Third Age. She admits that all this "seems like a miracle."

A Century of Wisdom is based on Alice's memories as related to me in countless hours of conversations and filmed interviews from 2004 to 2011. To know Alice is to see the world anew through the eyes of a woman who has lived for more than a century. Persistently independent today, Alice is supremely optimistic at an age far exceeding the norm. Her curiosity and emotional energy inspire all who have the good fortune to meet her. A student of philosophy, she has practiced what the philosophers taught. Particularly important to her is the ancient Greek stoic Epictetus, who wrote, "He is a wise man who does not grieve for the things which he has not, but rejoices for those which he has."

I have learned a great deal from Alice, who sees our human frailties and triumphs with equanimity and unique clarity from her vantage point of advanced age. The optimism and profound humanistic values she learned as a child, which govern the rhythm of her being, have never forsaken her in more than a century. Her story could be our textbook for living a far richer life. Surely it is the key to staying young.

A Century *of* Wisdom

ONE

Alice and Franz Kafka

As she unlatched the garden gate, eight-year-old Alice caught her first glimpse of a tall, very thin young man who, many years later, would be known as one of the greatest writers of the twentieth century. Franz Kafka was Uncle Franz to Alice. He had arrived in a horse-drawn cart with a little bunch of multicolored flowers for her mother. As the flowers wilted in the sun, Kafka stopped to feed the horse apples that had fallen to the ground. "Poor Franz," Alice reminisces. "He apologized for the flowers. But not because of their sad state but because there were so many different colors. He said he just couldn't decide which color to choose."

Alice had two older brothers, Georg and Paul, and two sisters, Irma, who was twelve years older than Alice, and Marianne, nicknamed Mitzi, who was Alice's twin. Irma had become engaged to Felix "Fritz" Weltsch, an outgoing young philosopher who had met Kafka when they both were studying law at Charles University. Rejecting law as their profession, they became fast friends when they worked together in the same insurance firm. Away from work Weltsch pursued a second doctorate in philosophy, while Kafka wrote and began to publish, and together with Max Brod and Oscar Baum they formed a writers' group, the "Prague Four." Later they befriended a teenage poet, Franz Werfel.

It was only natural that Weltsch would invite his best friend to meet his future in-laws. "He very often came to our house," Alice explains. Kafka felt so at ease in the Herzs' literary and musical home that he became a regular at their Sunday table. "He was [like] a member of our family," Alice says. Struggling with his Jewish identity, he found the warmth of their secular German Jewish life reassuring. Throughout his life Kafka settled on a kind of middle road with regard to his Jewish heritage, living by Jewish values, without adherence—other than his Bar Mitzvah—to organized religious traditions. He presented himself to the world and to his friends as a member of the European bourgeoisie, impeccably mannered and properly dressed. It is nearly impossible to find a photograph of Kafka casually clothed. As a child Alice thought it was strange that Franz always looked dressed for the office even on outings or picnics.

Observant Alice was quick to analyze and accept Kafka's ways. He could be depended on to be late, to forget something, and even to lose his way—and then he would arrive apologizing for all of the above. He was so apologetic that it felt to Alice as if he were apologizing for the food he ate or even for simply being alive. But once he got past this, he was a lot of fun, and very responsible with children. In summers Kafka, who was fond of swimming, would organize parties under the Charles Bridge. Alice and Mitzi were often invited, along with Irma and her fiancé. Long before she met Kafka, Alice had become a superb swimmer and had no difficulty racing across the Vltava River.

One of Alice's most endearing memories of Kafka was the cloudless summer day he showed up unannounced at their country house on the nanny's day off. The twins were fidgety and impatient; they wanted to explore the nearby forest or go somewhere for a picnic. Kafka suggested a walking expedition in the surrounding countryside. Sofie reluctantly gave her permission, and with Alice and Mitzi as companions, Kafka took off for an adventurous day of exercise and fun. He was a speed walker, having taken up the sport to build strength in his frail body. The little girls did their best to keep up, but after the first mile, they had to slow down and then stop for a break. Kafka found a log the twins could use for a bench and a tree stump for himself. From his perch he commanded their attention with stories about fantastic imaginary beasts. The more they laughed the wilder Kafka's inventions became. After an hour or so he produced "magic" sandwiches and a thermos of tea, which he claimed an invisible animal, half-bear and half-goat, had left for them in the woods. The great writer-to-be had as much fun as his charges.

Alice would always remember Franz Kafka as an "eternal child."

From the age of nine Alice would sit beside her mother and listen to Kafka talk endlessly about the book he was writing or the one he wanted to write. Her mother was fascinated with the writer's gifts, as literature and music had become an escape from her unhappy arranged marriage. Sofie was particularly intrigued by Kafka's opening sentences, which were modern, even revolutionary in the early years of the twentieth century. He began his novel *The Trial* with "Someone must have slandered Josef K., for one morning, without having done anything wrong, he was arrested." *The Metamorphosis* begins with "When Gregor Samsa woke up one morning from unsettling dreams, he found himself changed in his bed into a monstrous vermin." And *The Castle* draws the reader in with "It was late evening when K. arrived."

Alice would beg him to tell her the stories over and over again. But she always wanted to know the ending—and that he could not answer. He simply could not complete his work. Later on he would write, "I am familiar with indecision, there's nothing I know so well, but whenever something summons me, I fall flat, worn out by half-hearted inclinations and hesitations over a thousand earlier trivialities."

When Alice and her mother asked him why he went to law school and became an attorney if he did not want to practice law, Kafka's answer was simply that he could not decide what to study. He made this doubly clear when, after quitting Richard Lowy's law firm, he wrote, "It had never been my intention to remain in the legal profession. On October 1, 1906, I entered his service and remained there until October 1, 1907."

One year Kafka celebrated Passover with the Herz family. Despite his distaste for observing such traditions, he found Passover with Alice's relatives a joyful family affair. He seemed to tolerate and even accept in the Herz home precisely what he despised in his own family, especially his father's hypocritical annual practice of Jewish traditions. In *A Letter to His Father,* Kafka wrote, "I could not understand how, with the insignificant scrap of Judaism you yourself possessed, you could reproach me. . . . Four days a year you went to the synagogue, where you were . . . closer to the indifferent than to those who took it seriously."

At holiday time Sofie's Orthodox mother, Fanny, who lived with them, took over the kitchen and did her best to observe the Passover traditions. With the help of the maid, Fanny made kosher chicken soup, matzo balls, and the most tender brisket of beef. A few days before the holiday, she disposed of all leftover breads and pastries made with yeast and cleaned the cooking utensils, plates, and glasses with boiling water. Sofie and the children helped with the housecleaning. They polished the silver and set out their finest table linens. Alice was the most industrious, working hard to gain both her mother's and her grandmother's approval.

Alice's father, who was usually excessively frugal, opened his home to friends—gentiles, neighbors, strangers, and the poor—for the holiday, in keeping with the tradition. He also invited the most senior of his factory workers to share in the seder feast. In 1912, the year that Kafka probably participated, the Herz seder was one of their largest and, aside from the family and Felix, included Kafka, neighbors, several factory workers, and the writer Oskar Baum. Irma cautioned Alice to treat Baum, who was blind, just like anyone else. Much later, when Max Brod wrote about Kafka's first meeting with Baum, Alice recognized her sister's advice as a seminal moment in her moral education. As Brod was introducing them, Kafka silently bowed to Baum, greeting the blind man as an equal. "That was what he was like," Baum said. "Superior in depth of humanity to the ordinary run of kindness."

Alice does not recall all who came for the holiday that year. What she remembers is folding the snow-white linen napkins, so she knows there were many guests at the table that evening. Alice also thinks that Kafka asked her to sit next to him.

It was the duty of Alice and Mitzi to distribute the Haggadoth, the booklets recounting the story of Passover. Friedrich Herz, who had also been raised Orthodox, led the abridged readings in German; Alice and Mitzi, who were the youngest, read the four questions together; their father explained the ancient meaning of Passover; and Kafka helped the girls search for the afikomen. They all repeated the ancient text "This year we are here, next year in Jerusalem." No one, with the possible exception of Kafka, could have imagined that Jerusalem would become their safe haven in less than thirty years. When their father led "Dayenu," the children's favorite Passover song, in his rich baritone voice, everyone, even Kafka, sang. When the men retired to the living room for fine French brandy and cigars, they asked eight-year-old Alice to play. She obliged with a bagatelle by Beethoven and a Chopin waltz.

Kafka frequently fell in love. Although he made it clear that he dreamed of marriage, he complained that no one understood him. "To have one person with this understanding, a woman for example, . . . would mean to have God," he wrote in his diary. He was not looking for a wife who insisted on crystal chandeliers and—as Alice says—"that heavy German furniture." But Alice and her mother were certain that he would never decide to marry. He introduced Felice Bauer to them as his fiancée, then broke off the engagement only to get engaged to her a second time—for just a few weeks, until he changed his mind again. Hoping to comfort him, Alice's mother suggested to Kafka that he, like Beethoven and Brahms, was an artist and that he belonged to the world rather than to one woman.

But that was before Dora. Both Alice and her mother felt that twenty-five-year-old Dora Diamant was a different and affirmative presence in his life. Alice's mother said Franz had found his own true nature in Dora, and she hoped he would marry her. Thinking back to those days, Alice feels that her mother was instinctively right. Kafka was attracted to Dora's independent spirit as well as her motherly gentleness. Watching her scaling and gutting fish in the kitchen of a summer camp, he disapprovingly blurted out, "Such gentle hands and such bloody work." Dora was embarrassed. Brod revealed, "That was the beginning of his friendship with Dora Diamant, his life's companion."

Like Kafka's mother, Dora had been raised Orthodox, but like Kafka, she had escaped from her family's plans for her life. Even though Kafka had suffered through his Bar Mitzvah in 1896, he had since declared himself an atheist and a socialist. Dora's family had insisted that she marry early and aspired for her to be a wife and mother. Dora literally ran away from home to Berlin to get an education, and became a kindergarten teacher. She had leaned toward Zionism and shared Kafka's interest in Yiddish literature, later influencing his fascination with the Talmud. When she and Kafka began living together in Berlin, it was, they said, their first step toward a permanent home together in Palestine.

It was clear that Dora loved Kafka completely. When they first met and fell instantly in love, Kafka was forty years old, fifteen years older than Dora and already suffering with tuberculosis. As his disease soon required hospitalization, he was admitted to a sanatorium in Kierling, near Vienna. Alice remembers her mother's concern when Dora moved into Kafka's room to help care for him day and night. Miraculously, she never contracted tuberculosis. For a time he seemed to improve and even wrote cheerful letters to Alice's family. Even so, their time together was short-lived. Barely a year after their love affair started, on June 3, 1924, Kafka died, just as he was about to become famous.

Kafka's body was brought back to Prague for burial in Strašnice, the New Jewish Cemetery. Together with her entire family Alice attended his funeral in the cemetery chapel. Alice was nearly twenty-one by that time and well on her way to her own celebrity as a pianist.

Alice would see Dora once again—in 1950 in Israel, where Alice had immigrated after the war. Dora had settled in England, having escaped Stalin's Russia and Hitler's Holocaust; she had married and had a daughter. Because she had been an impassioned Zionist, Dora's single visit to Israel was a dream come true. Again Alice, Dora, and Felix Weltsch shared stories about Kafka, and pondered whether he would have been pleased or frightened by his posthumous fame. If he had lived, would he have agreed finally to marry Dora? Often calling herself Dora Kafka, Dora still believed that she would have been his wife, whereas Alice was certain he might have found some clever way out of the decision.

Alice has never stopped thinking about Kafka and his kindness to her. But why was he so indecisive? Why did he leave his books without endings? After many years of mulling it over, talking with Brod, and reading numerous books on Kafka, Alice has a theory—not found in any of the biographies of him she owns.

Alice explains that Kafka's mother was Orthodox, whereas his very strict and—according to Franz—somewhat cruel father was completely secular, maybe even an atheist. If Kafka practiced his mother's faith, he would face his father's wrath. And to renounce the religion of his mother and her ancestors would be to profoundly hurt the one who gave him life. Alice concludes, "Kafka never knew where he belonged, was never certain of his identity, or which path to take. To choose would mean that he would disappoint one of his parents. This, I think, was the core of his problem."

Alice notes that Kafka himself might be amused that scholars today debate his work in a Kafkaesque way. Some say his writings have nothing to do with Judaism or with his Jewish roots. Other scholars declare his work to be completely Jewish writing.

Alice accepts both verdicts as partially true.

INTERLUDE

An Emerald Ring

"He was not very beautiful—not good-looking at all," Alice muses. "But he was oh, so charming. Women were crazy for him." She is referring to Kafka's confidant and biographer Max Brod. Having known each other in Prague—Brod wrote rave reviews of Alice's first concerts and was a good friend of Alice's family—Alice and Brod reconnected as immigrants in Israel after Alice arrived in 1949.

Always a ladies' man, Brod was currently smitten with Annie, a red-haired young Russian woman. He had decided that this beauty should improve her piano skills under Alice's expert guidance. Because he was a friend and one of the few connections to her past life in Prague, Alice agreed to squeeze the unlikely student into her schedule.

During her second lesson the phone rang. It was Brod. "Is she still there with you?" he wanted to know. "Is she wearing a green ring? I gave her an emerald and I want to make certain that it is still on her finger!" Alice ran back to the piano, looked at the woman's hand, and saw that she had turned the ring so that it looked like a wedding band, with the small stone hidden in her palm. Later Brod admitted that he was trying to rehabilitate the lost soul and feared that she might have sold the ring for drugs on the way to her lesson.

This incident reminded Alice of the stories her brother Paul had told her of Brod's excursions with Kafka to Prague's exclusive brothels. *"Plus ça change, plus c'est la même chose."*

Alice smiled to herself and continued the lesson.

TWO

A Tolerant Heart

"I love people. All kinds of people. I love to talk with people." Alice tucks in her lips with an endearing grin. Then, closing her eyes for a moment as if searching for the right words, she clarifies her thoughts. "I don't look at people as a group to be judged. Behind every man and woman is a story. I am interested in learning about the best in each individual."

Alice tells stories of the Gypsy children who roamed Prague's streets when she was a child. Important friends of Alice's family often crossed to the other side of the road when they saw the five- and six-year-old Roma boys and girls approaching to beg for a few coins or chocolates. Alice was sternly warned to stay away from such people. "They are dirty and they steal."

"But they are smiling at us. Maybe they are hungry?"

Alice would reach out to them, and every time her mother or her father would pull her back, she felt wounded.

Later she would think of those same children when she would accompany a performance of Dvořák's *Gypsy Songs*, based on the exciting Roma folk music he loved. What if she were Roma? What was it like to be ostracized? Alice could never have believed then that she would find out firsthand. Nor could she have foreseen that her rights as a Czech citizen would be stripped away without recourse. Czechoslovakia was, after all, a free, democratic country with equal rights for all. Even capital punishment was nearly unknown.

Hitler hated the Jews even more than he despised the Gypsies. Everyone around Alice listened to the unsettling political news from Germany since Hitler had come to power. At first many Jews and gentiles alike did not take the inflammatory speeches, absurd racial laws, and hints of war too seriously. Many believed that the civilized, class-conscious Germans, with their enormous regard for university education, would never allow this impostor—a high school dropout who had lived in flophouses, not to mention never attended university—to lead a country that respected the aristocratic, highly educated Otto von Bismarck, who had unified the thirty-nine German states, as their ideal statesman. Convinced that the Germans would not put up with Hitler and his gang at the helm, many people assumed or tried to hope that the Nazi madness would quickly pass. And most decent people were unable to presume that Hitler was lying when he signed pacts and made promises to those whom he intended to destroy. Too many leaders in a position to make a difference in Britain, Europe, and America—including Churchill and Roosevelt—failed to recognize Hitler's evil genius until it was too late. When Vienna welcomed the German annexation of Austria, in 1938, with cheering, swastika-waving crowds, the optimists could no longer avoid the wake-up call. Jews all over Europe, desperate to escape, were urgently applying for visas to safe havens.

In 1938 Alice, at thirty-four years of age, had never been happier. She had everything she had ever wanted: she had given birth to her son the year before, she had a loving marriage, devoted students, and a promising career. Like many assimilated Jews, she and her husband still felt relatively safe under the Czechoslovak Army's protection. The Czech side of the border with Germany was heavily fortified, mountainous terrain. So when her friend Max Brod—who had been a committed Zionist for some years—began encouraging Alice and her sisters and their families to immigrate to Palestine with him, though her sisters decided to follow Brod, Alice felt compelled to stay in Prague. She and her husband did not want to risk resettling in a foreign land with such a young child; and although Alice's father had died of a heart attack nearly a decade earlier, her aging mother, whose ill health made it impossible for her to move abroad, needed Alice. Her eldest brother, Georg, who had led a decadent lifestyle of gambling and drinking, had died back in 1931 from the effects of alcoholism. And her other brother, Paul, subject to different racial laws because he was married to a Hungarian Catholic, had never settled on a profession. Both he and his wife loved gambling and were unreliable. Furthermore, Alice still believed in the promises of the treaty the British and French had made to protect her homeland.

Alice's mother sold most of her property to help with her sisters' expenses, and Alice also contributed a substantial part of her savings to help defray the cost of emigration. The British demanded a landing fee—equivalent to $100,000 in today's currency—for each person entering Palestine.

On September 29, 1938, determined to avoid a military encounter with Hitler, Britain's Prime Minister Neville Chamberlain and France's Prime Minister Édouard Daladier betrayed their treaty with Czechoslovakia in a joint meeting with the Führer in Munich. They agreed to Hitler's annexation of a large part of the Czech territory, known as the Sudetenland and home to 3 million citizens, in exchange for his promise that he would make no further territorial demands in Europe. Most historians agree that the combined Czech, French, and British forces could have soundly defeated the ill-equipped Germans, whose tanks broke down on the road to Prague, thus preventing further war in

Europe. But as the two heads of state sacrificed Czech democracy to the Nazi dictator, Chamberlain bragged that he had achieved "peace with honor, peace for our time." His moments of shameful glory were fleeting. The next day, October 1, Hitler's troops invaded the Sudetenland.

On a snowy March night in 1939, Max Brod and Alice's sisters, along with their families, boarded the very last train to leave Prague before the German occupation. Bound for Naples, where they would take a boat to Palestine, the train trudged across Czechoslovakia toward the Sudetenland. In the middle of the night it stopped on the Czech side of the German border, which was already occupied by Nazi troops. SS guards, guns drawn, inspected the train, car by car before the train continued.

The following day, March 15, it continued to snow heavily in Prague; the city looked dreary and was abnormally quiet. With Beneš and members of the free Czech government working in exile in England, where Czech soldiers and paratroopers had joined the British forces, Czechoslovakia was undefended. Hitler's troops, accompanied by Nazi tanks and trucks filled with soldiers waving their flags, marched into Prague unhindered. Czechoslovakia was no more. It had forcibly become a protectorate of greater Germany and was subjected to strict enforcement of the hostile racial laws imposed by the Nazi Reich.

In Prague, women allegedly lay down in the snow in a

futile effort to stop the tanks. Others sang the stately Czech anthem, with tears streaming down their faces. Alice listened to the news on the radio. Later she watched from the windows of a friend's house in the center of the city, near Wenceslas Square. The next day she stood in the crowd as Adolf Hitler himself entered her city. She quickly walked the two miles home to play with her two-year-old child.

Alice was now faced with people who were open enemies of all Jews; she could see even some of her gentile friends and neighbors turn away from her in fear for their own lives. By 1941, Leopold had been fired from his job in the import-export business because he was Jewish. Rafi was forbidden to attend a Czech nursery school or to play with non-Jewish children. Jews could not own telephones, radios, or bicycles. All Jews had to wear the yellow star stitched onto their clothing.

For a while many of Alice's non-Jewish piano students ignored the Nazi regulations and continued their lessons. But with each passing week this defiance became increasingly dangerous for both students and their teacher. Sadly they parted. Alice's meager income was reduced. The remaining Jewish pupils appeared at their usual times, finding comfort in the warmth of Alice's encouragement until they were deported.

Several Nazi families had moved into Alice's building. When Rafi was four years old he would play with Johann

Hermann, who was five and lived in an apartment on the floor above. Both shared their best toys, books, and their mothers' home-cooked soup. Both spoke German, dressed in short pants, and were on the chubby side. The children would play in the hallway, never in each other's apartments.

Sometimes at midday, when no one was around, Mrs. Hermann, a subservient housewife who cooked wonderful smelling dishes with ingredients that were no longer available to ordinary Czechs, would watch over the two boys as they played hide-and-seek in the courtyard. On rainy days she would read to the boys in the stairwell as Alice practiced.

Mr. Hermann, a member of the Nazi Party, had been sent to Prague to work as a civil servant at Gestapo headquarters. He did not wear a uniform, but once Alice saw him giving the Nazi salute to an officer in front of their building. The neighbors rarely saw him. He seemed to travel only at night or in the early morning.

In 1941 Adolf Eichmann announced his plans for the "final solution" to his staff at a secret meeting in Prague. "The Jews of Bohemia and Moravia are being gathered in a transit camp for evacuation. . . . Theresienstadt can comfortably absorb 50–60,000 Jews [at one time]. From there they will be transported to the East." Alice's mother and Leopold's parents were among the first Czech Jewish citizens to receive their deportation notices to Theresienstadt, early in 1942.

Heartbroken, Alice walked with her mother to the deportation center. There they said goodbye. Alice watched as her mother disappeared into the massive crowd. "Never will I forget that sight of my disconsolate seventy-two-year-old mother walking away slowly without ever looking back. And I could do nothing. Nothing," she whispered. "It was the lowest point of my life."

Leopold in the meantime had been working for the Prague Jewish Council, which was under Nazi supervision. After his business had been forcibly closed in accordance with the new Nazi laws, Leopold had desperately tried to launch another firm in neutral Belgium. Once it was established, he had hoped to move his family to Brussels. His plan was aborted when Hitler's troops occupied Belgium, on May 10, 1940. Leopold's only option was to flee back to Prague. The Jewish Council offered the sole work open to him as a Jew. Leopold and his co-workers had no choice but to comply with the Gestapo's orders to compile the lists of people for deportation. Although his work might have kept his and Alice's names off the list for a time, there would come a day when the Jewish Council staff would be deported as well, and the office would be permanently closed. By 1943 Prague was nearly *Judenfrei* (free from Jews), and it was only a matter of time until Leopold and his family would be summoned. He kept the news from Alice for as long as possible.

Their letter was delivered by the regular postman. On

July 3, 1943, the Sommer family was summoned to the collection center for deportation to Theresienstadt.

They had two days left in Prague. How could she explain this to Rafi? Yet even then Alice refused to give in to hopelessness and depression. The Prague Jewish Council, in early 1942, had told Alice about the concerts performed for fellow prisoners in Theresienstadt. She comforted herself with a question. "If we can play concerts, how bad can it be?" Over the following two days, Alice practiced as if she were preparing for a major European concert tour. Without stopping to eat, she worked on Beethoven sonatas and Chopin études until, drained, she lay on the Biedermeier sofa to consider her unknown future.

Word spread fast of their deportation, and by the next day, a few friends and acquaintances dropped in to say goodbye, their relief visible: it was she, and not they, who was being shipped off. Paul and his wife, Mary, spent a few private moments with Alice before a final hug. She offered them everything in the apartment, but it was no use. Their place was too small for extra furniture and besides, since Paul was Jewish, they had to be careful. No one asked Alice how she felt. No one brought goulash for supper. No one asked her to play. Like prospective buyers at an auction, they surveyed the apartment, wandering from room to room, opening closets and cupboards. The landlord joined the visitors as they began clearing things out. No one asked Alice if they could or should take this table or that set of dishes. One woman took a painting from the wall. Another grabbed an antique vase. A neighbor walked out of the bedroom with a gold necklace she found. Another neighbor from across the street grabbed it from her. "That is mine. Alice promised that I could take care of it."

Alice watched as they took whatever they could carry out of her apartment—supposedly for safekeeping. While some were carting household goods down to the street, the landlord fought with others for the carpets and chairs. Alice knew she would never see her belongings again. The Nazis would confiscate her piano, her most valuable possession of all, when they investigated the apartment after she and her family were gone. By the next day the Sommers would have no name and no citizenship. They would henceforth be known by their deportation numbers: DE 166, DE 167, and DE 168. On July 5, 1943, they would be shipped to Theresienstadt.

Very late that evening, after most residents were safely asleep, the Hermanns knocked on the door. "We brought a cake for your journey," Mrs. Hermann told Alice. It was an applesauce cake still warm from the oven and decorated with slices of sugary baked apples scented with cinnamon and cloves. Alice understood the exceptional wartime generosity of the cake rich with fresh eggs, butter, and precious sugar. Mr. Hermann could have been severely punished, for any kindness to Jews was strictly forbidden.

As Alice invited them into her apartment, Mr. Hermann glanced out the window to make certain no one was watching. Alice apologized that she had no chairs to offer. The Hermanns sat on the floor and asked her if she would play for them. Alice complied with Chopin's Nocturne in B-flat Minor, the first movement of Beethoven's sonata, opus 81a, titled *Das Lebewohl*—or *Farewell*—and, finally, the lyrical third étude of Chopin.

"Thank you, Mrs. Sommer," Mrs. Hermann said. "We will miss your music. We've loved listening to you practice. You made life easier for us during these hard times. Please take care and come back safely. Maybe our son can study piano with you someday." Then Mr. Hermann gave the soccer ball the boys played with to Alice. "I heard that your Rafi is fond of ball games," he said.

They did not shake hands, but Alice was nearly certain she saw a tear forming in Mrs. Hermann's eye as they turned to leave.

At Theresienstadt, husbands and wives were separated at the gate, so Leopold was rushed off to the men's section. As Alice was swept up in the crowds of displaced people, she told Rafi, "Hold my hand and don't let go! And remember, speak only Czech. Pretend you don't understand German." For the first time in her life she was terrified—frightened of losing her rambunctious six-year-old boy. "How could this nightmare be happening to us?" she asked herself repeatedly.

As she participated in concert after concert, Alice began to notice Nazi soldiers standing at the back of the room or listening from outside the windows. She could not help but wonder about those young, sometimes beautiful men wearing the burnished black boots and gray jackets emblazoned with Nazi emblems that to her symbolized death. Who were their mothers and fathers? Why were they here? How could they love music and still wear the swastika and serve evil? Some of their faces bore the unfurrowed brows and obedient bewilderment of those young Czech boys who had fled to England to join the fight. They were barely beyond childhood. Did they really hate Jews? Were they volunteers, or had they been forced into service? Did they believe the propaganda? Or were they, as she was, just hoping to survive and return home?

As the months passed, several of those young faces became familiar; Alice even saw one applaud until he was poked by his colleague as a reminder that appreciation of anyone or anything Jewish was forbidden. Late one evening as she was leaving the Magdeburg Barracks to make her way back to her quarters, a young officer approached her. He was tall and remarkably thin. His straight blond hair was longer than most soldiers'. To Alice he had the look of an aspiring poet. "Please," he told her, "I must say thank you. Your piano playing is magnificent." Alice looked at him and nodded her gratitude. Both disappeared into the darkness.

Alice later chided herself for not thanking the young man for daring to speak to her. Fraternization was subject to severe punishment. Alice was also aware that her fellow prisoners would be bitter toward her if they observed her extending any civility to their Nazi captors. But that night she decided that she had to remain true to herself. She would treat all equally. If a Nazi gave her a word of praise, she would thank him just as she would anyone else.

Nearly a year after her first encounter with the Nazi soldier, Alice played an exceptionally inspired concert of works by Beethoven, and afterward, another young soldier waited for her in the darkness of a doorway. His voice startled her. "Are you Mrs. Sommer, the pianist?"

Continuing to walk, Alice answered, "Yes, I am Mrs. Sommer."

"A moment please," he commanded.

Alice stopped as a man nearly twice her height blocked her way. "I must speak to you. Do not be afraid."

Alice looked him straight in the face and responded, "What do you want?"

"Frau Sommer," he continued in German, "I come from a musical family. My mother was a fine pianist. She took me to many concerts. I understand very much about music. I only want to thank you for your concerts. They have meant much to me."

Alice smiled as she whispered, "Thank you. I am glad that the music helps you." In those few seconds she had seen a frightened young man who might have been her friend if they were not separated by the uniform he wore. "I must go."

Looking around to see that they were not observed, he said, "Please, one more thing. You and your little son will not be on any deportation lists. You will stay in Theresienstadt until the war ends. Do not worry, you will be safe." With those words he quickly disappeared.

Alice never saw him again. Nor does she know his name or rank. Was he sent to the front? Did he survive?

After the war the Nazi deportation lists to Auschwitz were discovered in the archives of war records. Neither Alice's name nor the name of her child could be found on any of the final lists.

Alice has always wondered what the cost may have been to the young Nazi who she believes saved her life, and also what happened to the Hermanns—and, if they survived the war, what became of their son. More than half a century later, memories of these individuals continue to haunt her.

THREE

Peeling Potatoes

That Alice would become friendly with Golda Meir, the carpenter's daughter from Milwaukee who became Israel's prime minister, should not be surprising. Alice, like Golda, had no use for material or frivolous values, and they shared a disdain for pretension and a commitment to the moral life above ambition. The war years had proved what she could live without, having been robbed of everything except what was in her mind. "Only what is inside is important," she often says.

With her socialist soul rooted in kibbutz life, Golda Meir did not seem to change as her political life gained momentum, from being ambassador to the Soviet Union to foreign minister to first female prime minister of Israel. Despite her reputation as a tough leader, Golda never suppressed her joy or her sadness. "It's no accident many accuse me of conducting public affairs with my heart instead of my head," she said in an interview with Oriana Fallaci. "Well, what if I do? . . . Those who don't know how to weep with their whole heart don't know how to laugh either," she said. Many talk about the authentic life. Both Alice and Golda lived it.

Alice no longer remembers where she first met Golda, but she thinks it must have been at the Jerusalem Academy of Music, years before Golda became prime minister. Alice recalls a tall, strong-looking woman in a print dress buttoned up to her neck who complimented her in Yiddish after a concert. Never would she forget that woman's description, "ravishingly beautiful," of Schumann's *Fantasy* in C Major, Opus 17, that Alice had just performed, and that more than once she would ask Alice to play it for her. Alice was strongly drawn to the piece as well. "There were moments in that piece so achingly beautiful that they simply broke my heart," she says. Their first meeting probably occurred in late 1949, after Golda returned from Moscow, where she had served as Israel's first ambassador to the Soviet Union. Golda had undoubtedly heard about Alice Herz-Sommer because of the many concerts she had played in the concentration camp.

When Alice arrived in Israel in March 1949 with her son, she moved in with her sister Mitzi, but soon she was able to find her own apartment in Jerusalem. It was there she began a tradition of hosting Sunday afternoon musicales. This was a sure way to bring together not only her new friends but also her relatives and old friends—a way to revive her memories of her life in Prague. A psychiatrist had suggested to Alice that a home frequently filled with family and friends was a helpful antidote to the strangeness of a new country and the inevitable loneliness of her only child. An adept page turner, Rafi could always be found in the middle of the entertainment, extending his services during the performances of chamber music.

Alice had no telephone and no time to write invitations, but in those years in Jerusalem word of mouth was more than sufficient. In addition to the core group of her two sisters and their husbands, Max Brod and Edith Kraus—a pianist who had survived Theresienstadt and Auschwitz—were nearly always present. If enough players for chamber music did not show up, Edith or Alice would offer solo piano works. And if too many people found their way to Alice's "Sundays," the door to the apartment would be left open to accommodate the latecomers in the hallway. Seated on the floor, they would still be able to listen to the music. Alice's only caveat was that her visitors must never ask her questions about or speak of the Holocaust in her home. The years from the time they were deported by the Nazis until they arrived in Israel were not topics for conversation.

Golda Meir lived nearby in the friendly neighborhood. Frequently, Alice's students reported seeing her when they were on their way to classes. Having learned about the weekly gatherings from Brod, one winter Sunday in the early 1950s, Golda appeared a quarter of an hour early, curious to get better acquainted with the self-effacing pianist from Czechoslovakia.

The night before, Alice had prepared a huge pot of goulash soup, a dish that she could assemble quickly and that would cook slowly while she slept. When Golda walked in, Alice was hurrying to peel a mountain of potatoes. At first Alice noticed only the feet clad in heavy, black orthopedic shoes making tracks in the water that had dripped onto the kitchen floor. In the same moment that she said "Shalom," Golda grabbed a towel and wiped up the mess she had made. Without missing a beat Alice pointed down to her own canvas sneakers. "It seems that we have happy feet," she said. Both women laughed, knowing how most women's feet hurt from their fashionable high heels, unaware then that "Golda's shoes" would one day become a euphemism for all that was ugly and old-fashioned. Then, without asking, Golda grabbed a knife from the counter and began to peel the potatoes like a professional sous-chef. Alice did not protest.

Neither woman wore makeup, and both were dressed in simple cotton skirts and blouses. Both lived in the Rechavia district near the Old City. Their first bits of conversation sounded as if they had taken up from where they last left off. "I hope you don't mind that I am early. I love to help." "Don't you want something to drink, coffee?" "Did you see the article in today's paper about Yehudi Menuhin?" "Of course, did you hear the concert?"

Golda had been instrumental in providing major government assistance to the refugees, and she inquired if she could help Alice in any way. Alice responded with grateful appreciation for their safe haven. "Do you have children, did they survive?" Golda asked. Alice offered to introduce Golda to her teenage son, who played both cello and piano. Golda, who was five years older than Alice, talked of raising her two children on the kibbutz and how helpful the community had been for working mothers. "What happened to your child, where was he during the Holocaust? Was he hidden?" she asked.

Alice paused for a moment, looked Golda straight in the eyes, and said, "I never talk about that time. I do not want anyone to pity me. I do not want my son to remember. I want his childhood to be happy." Golda seemed sympathetic to her response but pressed on. "But how do you feel about the Germans and all that happened to our people?" At first Alice remained silent. Then she said, "I am not here to discuss the past. I love this young country, where maybe I can contribute. I was not spared to spend my days looking back, to make myself and others miserable. And soon we will make beautiful music." And then Alice remembers hearing Golda say, "Peeling potatoes gives me *naches* (joy)."

That day in Alice's kitchen a friendship was cemented.

Alice's and Golda's lives had many similarities. Both were single mothers of gifted sons who studied the cello. Menahem Meir and Rafi Sommer, though thirteen years apart in age, both had the great fortune to study with the world's greatest cellist, Pablo Casals. Both became highly respected performers, concertizing widely. Later on Menahem would become director of the Israel Conservatory of Music in Tel Aviv, while Rafi took a position as professor of cello at Guildhall School of Music in London. Alice once explained to Golda that her father had not been educated and had never read great books either; still, the women agreed that they had absorbed more about life from their fathers than from their mothers. And each had chosen to live without a husband. Golda's marriage had fallen apart because of the time and effort she devoted to her work, and although Alice did not lack for suitors, she never remarried; once she was in Israel, no man could distract her from her life in music.

As the years passed and Golda rose to more powerful government positions, the two women saw far less of each other. When Golda was foreign minister, she traveled continually. Alice, meanwhile, was consumed with raising Rafi and teaching, practicing four or more hours each day and traveling around Israel for her concerts.

Alice was not surprised when Golda became the first female prime minister. She felt that Golda was the best choice for the job and that she had earned "her promotion." Today Alice fondly says, "You could trust her as a world leader— she had common sense, she loved people, she worked for peace, but was tough when she needed to be."

Word was spreading about Alice's frequent concerts in Jerusalem and Tel Aviv, and more and more of Israel's elite could be spotted in her audiences. She soon attracted the greats of the country to her home as well as to her performances. Max Brod served as her chronicler and showed Alice the lists he made of her well-known admirers: Leonard Bernstein, Isaac Stern, Abba Eban, Arthur Rubinstein, Yehudi Menuhin, Zubin Mehta, the young Daniel Barenboim, and, along with Golda, Teddy Kollek, the future beloved mayor of Jerusalem. Alice says, "Kollek was always gracious and charming, but Golda was very musical. She had not had the opportunity to study, but by going to concerts frequently she taught herself to listen. Golda understood the music's message. But Kollek, not so much." Alice mentioned that sometimes she thought Kollek had fallen asleep during a concert.

According to Alice and others, Golda had high musical standards. Isaac Stern, Rudolf Serkin, and Arthur Rubinstein were frequent guests in her home. Proud of her role as honorary president of the famous Rubinstein International Piano Master Competition, she said, "Although I don't know much about music, I love and have a special affinity for three musicians, for Casals, for Rubinstein, and for my son!" Alice protests Golda's understated self-assessment. "But Golda was very knowledgeable," she insists. "She knew a lot about music."

When the Israel Philharmonic came into being as the Palestine Philharmonic Orchestra, in 1936, Golda was in the audience at its first concert. Conducted by Arturo Toscanini, a refugee himself from fascist Italy, the concert was held in a large pavilion at the Tel Aviv fairground. Maestro Toscanini, recognized at the time as the world's greatest conductor, said, "It is the duty of everyone to fight and help in this sort of cause according to one's means." He declined payment from the Palestine Symphony, even for travel expenses, with the explanation that he was "doing this for humanity," in solidarity with the musicians who had been victimized by the Nazis.

Golda had met the orchestra's founder, the violinist Bronisław Huberman, when he sat next to her on a flight from Los Angeles to San Francisco in the mid-1930s, while she was in the United States on a mission for Histadrut (the Jewish Labor Federation). He had told her of his plans to establish a symphony orchestra in Palestine where the Jewish musicians who were fleeing Germany would be able to play, and she had vowed to help him. Golda later admitted to her son that she had felt flattered that such an enormously famous violinist had recognized her.

Huberman had performed Brahms's Concerto for Violin in Vienna with the composer seated in the hall. In 1896, the year of his Carnegie Hall debut, the great composers of the world—Antonín Dvořák, Gustav Mahler, Anton Bruckner, and Johann Strauss, as well as Brahms—could be seen in his audiences. And now, with the help of Albert Einstein as head of American Friends of the Palestine Philharmonic, Huberman funded the orchestra as his contribution to the building of the future State of Israel. The first seventy-three members were all recent immigrants who had fled from Nazi Germany and Austria, many of whom had known Huberman before the war. Although Alice had never met him personally, she had heard him play several times in prewar Prague and Vienna.

Menahem Meir remembers that what was so meaningful about that first concert was that artists and audience alike had gathered against the background of the Arab riots that were being launched to protest Jewish immigration and the British Mandate. Precious trees and crops were destroyed, homes were burned to the ground, and nearly one hundred Jews—some who had been refugees from Hitler—had been killed. In his biography of his mother, Menahem wrote, "The fact that Toscanini and other gifted artists had knowingly and willingly entered this atmosphere to be with us, filled our hearts to overflowing."

Because of Golda's accidental meeting with Huberman during their flight, she was also able to talk him into sponsoring an annual series of concerts for factory workers and farmers. Golda and her family attended those programs, according to Menahem, with "nearly religious devotion."

Even after she became prime minister, Golda attended concerts whenever she could. Once she confessed to Alice that she had always longed to study piano. When she was a child in Milwaukee there was no money for lessons. And later, given her responsibilities as worker, wife, and mother, she had no spare time. She asked if Alice thought that she could still learn even though she was past her seventieth birthday. Alice told her, "It is never too late to try." "Alice," Golda said with unusual hesitance, "would you accept me as your student, teach me to play piano, when I retire?"

Alice pressed Golda's hand and said, "It will be my great joy to give lessons to you because you are so musical. How soon can we start?"

Sadly the piano lessons were never to be. Golda developed lymphatic cancer and died in 1978.

Today, nearly thirty years after Alice immigrated to England, she says that her happiest days were lived in Israel. "It was in Jerusalem that I watched my son grow strong and healthy without scars from the war years. I loved the many gifted students that I taught—Sabras, Palestinians, Russians, Americans. Israel represented both the past and the present. It was a time of great hope. Everything seemed possible."

Politically Golda held socialist values, whereas Alice, who knew little about politics, was simply detached from material possessions. Alice remembers the private moment when Golda, who had been raised Orthodox, asked her about religion. Golda smiled when Alice answered, "I am Jewish, but Beethoven is my religion."

Music, potato peeling, and love of Israel provided the bond that made the friendship possible between these two immigrant women—the pianist from Prague and the future prime minister of Israel.

INTERLUDE

Dreaming

Irma, Alice's older sister, who was a gifted pianist, gave Alice her first lessons at the age of seven. Whereas her twin, Mitzi, showed no particular affinity for the instrument, from the beginning Alice practiced endlessly, memorizing every piece she learned.

In late November before her ninth birthday she was able to give a credible performance of Robert Schumann's popular and gently evocative "Träumerei" (Dreaming). Alice played the piece over and over, trying to achieve her own interpretation. She practiced it very slowly and softly, and then decided it sounded more effective a bit faster and with a stronger melody line.

Her brother Paul, who was four years older and making serious progress as a violinist, wanted to play the beautiful "Träumerei" with Alice. He was haunted by its infectious melody and borrowed his sister's music for his next lesson. His teacher told him that the piece was written for piano not violin, and although Paul had turned it into a violin arrangement, the teacher did not believe that one so young could understand such romantic music. "Do you know what love feels like?" the teacher asked. "I do not mean love for your parents or your country, but romantic love for a woman?" Twelve-year-old Paul confessed that he thought of the sister of his best friend every morning and every evening and sometimes even during his math classes. "Yes, I know love, my heart beats fast every time I think of her. Sometimes I can barely breathe." The teacher then agreed that he could try "Träumerei."

That evening at home, Paul asked Alice to play it with him. Excessively exaggerating his feelings, Paul could not keep the rhythm. Alice corrected him. "But you do not know love. You are too young. I am expressing the feeling behind the music," he replied. She quickly retorted, "I may be younger than you, but I know how to count, and to play what the composer wrote."

FOUR

Piano Lessons

"Music was always all around me. I mean live music, people playing or singing, not recordings. That came years later." Alice is referring to some of her fondest childhood memories. "My mother was a marvelous pianist." Nodding her head, she adds, "*Ja, ja,* how she loved to play. It was one of her diversions from melancholy."

In Prague, nearly everyone Alice knew owned a piano, but the one in her house seemed to reign over her family's living room. It was a large grand—or at least it appeared to be enormous to young Alice—that had belonged to her grandmother. The keyboard was always covered when not in use, and no one was allowed to open it or to touch its keys without first washing their hands. Alice and Paul would often give informal performances before bedtime. Alice would play waltzes by Chopin and Strauss, pieces from Schumann's

Kinderscenen, and early sonatas by Beethoven. Together she and Paul would offer movements of Mozart's or Schubert's sonatas for violin and piano. They had great fun performing Dvorak's Sonatina for violin and piano, based on Native American melodies the composer heard in America. Sofie found the music rather exotic. Often their concerts ended with Dvořák's familiar "Humoresque." Alice can still hear the neighbors calling, "Hurry, the Herzes are about to begin."

In 1910, when Alice began her piano lessons, music was in the Prague air. "In those beautiful years," Alice reminisces, "Prague was music." The green and gold jewel box theater where Mozart had conducted the premiere of *Don Giovanni* stood majestically in the center of the city, just off Old Town Square. Alice's older sister, Irma, had shown it to the twins many times on their walks, reminding them that Prague was Mozart's favorite city. She took them on picnics to the farmhouse Bertramka, where Mozart had lived with his wife when he was writing the overture to *Don Giovanni.* Inside the house Alice was allowed to touch the tiny piano with soft, bell-like tones that Mozart had played little more than a century earlier.

Musicians, past and present, were revered. Bedřich Smetana and Antonín Dvořák had put the Czechs on the world map with their music inspired by national folk tunes. The greatest artists of the day performed in Prague. Concerts and operas often made front-page news in the morning papers and were not to be missed. Even the poor and uneducated could be found in the standing-room sections when the tickets were sold out. "Sometimes we saved for months in order to afford the ticket for an important concert," Alice says.

Civil servants, bankers, businessmen, doctors, lawyers, housewives—many of them were highly skilled amateur musicians, and those who were not competent instrumentalists sang in choruses. Their weekly rehearsal time was sacrosanct. The word *amateur* is derived from the Latin word *amator,* lover, and music was, for many, their grandest love affair. House concerts, called *Hauskonzerte,* whether performed by professionals or amateurs, were a popular form of entertainment; in fact, friends would frequently gather in someone's home to hear the first performance of a new work with the composer in attendance.

Beyond her musical gifts, Alice was an ideal pupil. Irma instilled in her a love of practicing. Alice made corrections easily and gratefully, repeating a phrase or section until she mastered the task at hand. Perhaps because Alice was more than eleven years younger, Irma never seemed jealous of her sister's abilities. Instead she found reward in the praise she garnered for being such a fine teacher. After two years, Irma introduced Alice to her former teacher, Václav Štěpán, who was considered Prague's finest pedagogue. Alice played a

movement of a Beethoven sonata for Štěpán, who com-
mended both the child and the teacher. Although he did not
normally teach young children, Štěpán was so moved by Alice's passion for playing that he agreed to see her once each
month, while Irma would continue the weekly lessons and
supervise Alice's practicing. A couple of years later Štěpán
began to teach Alice in earnest; he would become her mentor and constant friend.

It was a time when Alice could learn from those who
were only one generation removed from the immortals. She
could literally touch the hands of those who had been close
to Brahms, Liszt, and Chopin. Her future teacher at the
academy, Conrad Ansorge, had studied piano with the tech-
nical wizard Franz Liszt. Johannes Brahms had given his
own grand piano to his student Alexander Zemlinsky, the
inspired founder of Alice's conservatory, who became her
friend. In concerts she learned from the pianists Wilhelm
Backhaus and Moriz Rosenthal, who had been taught by
Chopin's most promising pupil, Karol Mikuli.

Even though Alice graduated from the Prague German
Conservatory of Music as a student of Ansorge, it was Štěpán
who continued to guide her career. He arranged for her
debut as a soloist with the Czech Philharmonic, coached her
performance of Chopin's E-minor Concerto, accompanied
Alice to the rehearsals, and invited Max Brod to attend the

concert. Spellbound by the young pianist's otherworldly tone and impeccable technique, Brod wrote a glowing review of her performance. It would be the first of many. Recalling those days, Alice says that, when she played in Prague, she always cast a quick sidelong glance to see if Max was in his usual seat. Only when she knew that he was in the hall could she begin. When questioned about stage fright, Alice simply has nothing to say because she never experienced it. "Stage fright comes mainly from caring more about what others think than about the music itself," she says. "The only possible fear that I might have had was of my own inner critic. But once I began to play, even that anxiety disappeared."

After her early successes, she registered for seminars with the well-known pianist Eduard Steuermann, who announced that he would travel from Vienna to Prague to teach the most gifted students there. Steuermann's fees were required in advance for his twelve master classes, but Alice was bitterly disappointed by the cold and uncaring attitude he demonstrated toward the students. She felt that she learned nothing musical from him and had wasted her money and her time. She later walked away equally disappointed from an hour lesson with the famous Artur Schnabel that had cost her an entire month's salary. Ultimately Alice learned to trust her own judgment, and in the process, she learned to teach others. For Alice, a performance career and all that it entailed was secondary to a life as a dedicated artist in search of excellence.

Nearly one year after the Nazi invasion of Prague, on Sunday, March 3, 1940, Alice participated in a secret concert of new works by the Jewish composer Viktor Ullmann in the home of Konrad Wallerstein. She fondly recalls, "Their home was so *gemütlich* [homey and warm]. And they had a beautiful Steinway." The living room was furnished with Biedermeier originals inherited from Mrs. Wallerstein's parents. Multicolored Persian carpets covered the floors. But the silver coffee service sat empty on the dining room sideboard, and the usual Czech tea cakes topped with bits of fruit were missing too. The small fire in the fireplace provided the only heat in the room. Everyone except the performers wore their coats and gloves all afternoon.

Alice played Ullmann's extremely modern and difficult Second Sonata for Piano that afternoon. After the performance the composer hugged Alice, and Wallerstein gave her one red rose in appreciation. No one knew how he had secured such a treasure. Three years later, in Theresienstadt, the composer would dedicate his newly written Fourth Sonata to Alice, but the Second would remain her favorite and the only one that she would ever play publicly.

All of the highly educated Czech citizens who had gathered for that concert spoke German as their language of choice. They bore German family names and had attended German schools. They had all defied the Nazi ban on Jews assembling together. Still hopeful that things would not get worse, they were unaware that everyone in that room would soon be torn from their homes and end up in Theresienstadt on their way to Auschwitz and other camps in the East.

Alice would be the only guest that day to survive.

INTERLUDE

Fire

"I was born an optimist, while my twin was always a pessimist. Very interesting," Alice says. "Mitzi was my mother's favorite because she was so small and weak. She was always waiting for catastrophes to happen."

When Alice was a child, her father frequently told a story about a fire in his factory that had a profound but different effect on each of the twins. A month or two before Alice and Mitzi were born, Friedrich Herz had eaten his hearty noon meal at home and retired for a nap—a habit of most businessmen at the time—before returning to his desk in the Herz Brothers Factory, which manufactured precision scales. Suddenly he was roused from sleep by shouts of "Fire, fire," coming through the open windows. The factory building stood less than two hundred yards from the

Herz family's home on the same property. Friedrich slipped into his shoes and ran outside to investigate. Seeing flames leaping from the plant, without a moment's hesitation he rushed inside to try to control the inferno. He quickly discovered a leaking gas pipe and disconnected it. When he emerged from the building, Friedrich looked as if he had been burned all over. His face, hands, and clothes were blackened almost beyond recognition. When he sat down on the bench to congratulate his workers, he realized that he was in considerable pain. Someone thrust a flask of whiskey into his hands, and others ran for a doctor. For once in his life Friedrich Herz drank liberally in an effort to numb his pain.

Sometimes when he retold the story, Friedrich made the children laugh as he described how he tried to run toward the factory with his pants falling down. When he had lain down after having eaten, he had only taken off his jacket and slipped his suspenders from his shoulders. In his excitement he had forgotten to pull the suspenders up again. But never once did he insert a note of fear into the story, for Friedrich Herz was instinctively a fearless man.

Alice says that, while listening to their father's story, Mitzi, an anxious child, imagined that he could have been burned alive. Alice, by contrast, felt proud that he had solved a problem and emerged a hero.

Alice believes that her father's example in such an extreme and life-threatening situation helped to cement her optimism as a child, and influenced the equanimity with which she approached decision making later on.

FIVE

Starting Over

When the Soviet Army liberated Theresienstadt, they simply told the inmates, "You are free, you can go home." They did not supply food, medical care, or transportation, because they had nothing to give and were ordered to join the liberation forces in Prague. Fortunately the Red Cross quickly intervened to care for those who had survived. Within a few days officials from the Jewish Agency also appeared. Alice learned from them that she could spend part of the summer recuperating on a farm nearer to Prague. Rafi would be able to celebrate his eighth birthday in June in freedom, play in the sunshine, eat fresh and healthy food, and together they could regain their strength. This seemed to her more sensible than rushing into an unknown situation in the city.

In late July 1945, Alice and Rafi finally made their way back to Prague. But returning Jews were unwanted there and at times faced malicious anti-Semitism; they found that ethnic Czechs refused to vacate the apartments they had seized, now claiming them as their property. Former Czech neighbors who had graciously offered to keep jewelry and valuable furniture safe were unpleasantly surprised when the Jews appeared on their doorsteps to claim them back. Most of the time they responded by angrily shutting their doors. The government offered little help.

As a non-Jew, Mary, Paul's wife, had been permitted to continue living in their small apartment while he was briefly interned in Theresienstadt in early 1945. Paul and his wife offered to share their two rooms with Alice and Rafi, but it was only a temporary solution. Alice had to find food and a place to live in her home city, where little more than two years earlier she had had an apartment, work, and savings. But the Nazis had obliterated all trace of Alice Herz-Sommer and had stolen her entire bank account. Another Czech family was inhabiting her former apartment and refused to move. All signs of her furniture, paintings, and antique porcelain had vanished. Although she looked for a few of the people who had promised to save her belongings, they were nowhere to be found. She would have to prove herself a Czech-born citizen by filing endless forms only to discover that she needed to complete still other forms in a truly Kafkaesque turn. In Theresienstadt she had instructed Rafi to speak only Czech so that the Nazis would not understand his words. Now that they were home, Alice had to tell her son once again never to speak German, since speaking it could be life threatening and all prewar German schools had been closed. Perhaps the words "You can't go home again" had never rung more true.

Alice began to find piano students, and she would run from house to house to teach, as she had no piano of her own. A few months later, with the help of the Red Cross and what was left of the Jewish community, she was able to secure a small apartment, and the Jewish Community Organization gave her the opportunity to choose a piano from their large storehouse of Nazi-confiscated instruments. Sadly, her own beautiful grand could not be located. After the piano was delivered to her new address, she touched it gently, wondering what had happened to its owner. Now that Alice had a piano, she was able to increase her teaching hours and to practice consistently for the day when she might again play publicly. The opportunity came when she was offered a concert for Czech radio to be broadcast internationally. Not only did she hope to reestablish her career but she also thought the concert would be a way to let her friends know that she had survived the war. Alice played Beethoven's *Appassionata* Sonata to signal her return.

As if their betrayal of Czechoslovakia at Munich had not done enough harm, the Allies continued to mandate postwar strategy. When Truman, Stalin, and Churchill met in 1945 in Yalta, they divided Europe into war zones to be liberated by British, American, or Soviet troops. Those same liberation forces would then control their zones and oversee the establishment of a civil government after the war. This decision was tragic for the countries that would soon fall under Soviet domination. Czechoslovakia was betrayed a second time when Churchill and Truman agreed to allow Stalin's Red Army to liberate Prague, thus sealing that country's communist future under Soviet control. General Patton marched into Czechoslovakia, near Marienbad, ahead of the Red Army, but was forced to abort his advance. He and his troops were ordered to halt in Pilsen until the Soviets could liberate Prague nearly a week later.

In one of the darkest periods in Czech history, the so-called Revolutionary Guards multiplied. Operating outside Czech laws, they sought to rid the nation of the German presence. Many of these Guards had been Nazi collaborators, brutal opportunists who had donned revolutionary hats only to hide their past. They ruthlessly hunted down anyone with German origins or cultural sympathies. Even the music of German composers, including Bach, Beethoven, and Brahms, was frowned upon.

Prewar Czechoslovakia had been a tolerant mix of Czechs, Germans, Jews, and Poles. Gypsies, however, experienced racial discrimination. Yet anyone born within its borders had been automatically granted citizenship. After Soviet troops had liberated Prague in May 1945, President Edvard Beneš returned to Czechoslovakia to issue decrees, which ultimately resulted in the expulsion of over two and a half million Sudeten Germans and more than a half million ethnic Hungarians, and the massacre of thousands of civilians. Mass graves of the victims are still being discovered. Nationalism prevailed over reason after Beneš said the age of minority rights was ended. Beneš and others talked openly about Czechoslovakia becoming a homogenous Czech state free from all minorities, provoking nearly three years of pitiless ethnic cleansing. He seemed to have forgotten the principles of the beloved first president of Czechoslovakia, Tomáš Garrigue Masaryk, which guaranteed protection of civil rights for all citizens.

Incited by President Beneš and raw memories of the brutal Nazi occupation, the Czechs turned against their own citizens in a barbaric frenzy. The worst of the nation's reign of terror continued from May 1945 until early 1947. Tens of thousands of ethnic Czech-Germans—who were native-born Czechoslovakian citizens, but ethnically Germanic— were forcibly removed from their homes and marched or taken in cattle cars to the German and Austrian borders, where they had neither food nor shelter. Many died on the way. Wanton rape of thousands of women, hideous torture, and murder were common aspects of daily life. A baker and his wife were shot dead in their shop because they did not give free bread to a Revolutionary Guard who accused them of being German. One journalist reported that he had seen a crowd watching two young men, still alive, hanging upside down from trees. Russians and Czechs carried gasoline containers from a nearby tank, and together they poured the gas over their victims and set them on fire. The journalist watched as onlookers lit their cigarettes from the human torches.

Alice was appalled by the cruelty the Czechs unleashed in their frenzy of ethnic cleansing. "Before the war, we—Czechs, Germans, Jews—were friends and neighbors. Most of us were bilingual. We had two mother tongues, Czech and German. We read both Czech and German newspapers. Kafka, Rilke, and many other great Czech authors wrote their books in German, while some, like Karel Čapek, wrote in Czech. Before the war we lived all together as Czechoslovaks."

President Beneš had rallied the patriots to action with one word, *Lidice.* In 1942 the Nazis had destroyed the village of Lidice, about one hour's drive from Prague, in retaliation for the assassination of Deputy Reichsprotektor SS General Reinhard Heydrich, the highest Nazi officer in Prague. On orders from Karl Hermann Frank, all 192 men over the age of sixteen were murdered by Nazi firing squads as they returned from work to their homes on June 10. The women and children were shipped to concentration camps, where most of them died. The residents of Lidice were all Catholic. The village was burned to the ground; the cemetery was dug up and its remains destroyed. Two weeks later, a second village, Ležáky, was similarly destroyed. The Nazis targeted these villages because they were suspected of hiding resistance fighters and their relatives. Although atrocities in the concentration camps and elsewhere were top secret, the Nazis proudly announced the massacre in Lidice as a warning to the Allies.

Many historians agree that without President Beneš's authoritative attitude toward the ethnic minorities, violence against citizens who bore German names would not have occurred. Recalling the postwar violence, Alice nods. "*Ja, ja,* we [Czechs] loved President Beneš, we looked up to Beneš. How could he, the successor to Masaryk, have compromised with Stalin?"

In the midst of this chaos and death, the NKVD (Soviet secret police), who also freely patrolled Prague after the Nazi surrender, arrested Michal Mareš, a gentile Czech journalist, in early May 1945. Ironically, the fact that Mareš was an idealistic member of the Czech Communist Party did not prevent the Soviets from dumping him into prison on vague, trumped-up charges. Mareš never knew why he had been targeted.

In solitary confinement, Mareš was told that he had received the death sentence and would be executed. Within a few days a group of soldiers removed him from his cell, marched him into an interior courtyard, bound him to a wall, blindfolded him, and shouted, *"Ogoň!"* (Fire!). The firing squad had been ordered to shoot into the air, and Mareš was not injured. After exchanging a vulgar joke, described by Mareš in his autobiography, the soldiers returned him to his cell. His fake execution, one of the Soviets' special forms of torture, was staged twice more. While he was still in prison, Revolutionary Guards murdered Mareš's helpless old father in his bed, mistaking him for a German. Mareš was released in Prague on the day his father was buried. His father's assassination opened Mareš's eyes to the truth of the Soviet system and its ultimate intentions.

Michal Mareš had been in love with Alice's playing and had frequented her concerts before the war. They had known each other because Mareš too had been friends with Kafka, Weltsch, and Brod. Mareš just happened to tune in to Alice's broadcast after her concert had started. Listening to his radio that Saturday night in September 1945, Mareš, now out of jail, wondered who the pianist with this deeply spiritual interpretation of the *Appassionata* Sonata might be. When the announcer identified the performer as Alice Herz-Sommer, Mareš was overjoyed. Alice was alive. The morning after the broadcast, he lost no time in visiting the Jewish Community

Center to try to learn where she was living. Stopping only to buy flowers, he rushed to her apartment.

For some time Alice had felt that her husband had not survived. She still looked for him day after day for many weeks after she returned to Prague. On the late summer day the Jewish Agency confirmed her instinct and she saw Leopold's name on the deceased list, Alice was not shocked; she had already accepted his fate. When Mareš appeared, Alice welcomed the attentions of her brilliant admirer. Mareš took on the role of surrogate father to eight-year-old Rafi and happily entertained him for hours while Alice taught or practiced. Mareš helped Rafi with his homework, took him to the cinema and out for as many flavors of ice cream as Rafi could eat.

Alice was attracted to Mareš's idealism. Well educated in the humanities and exceptionally knowledgeable about European classical music of the eighteenth and nineteenth centuries, Mareš was an experienced traveler who had not only toured Europe but also visited several African countries. When he was a teenager he had protested the murder of Francesco Ferrer, the anarchist teacher in Spain, and for this offense Mareš was banned from all schools in the Austro-Hungarian Empire. After World War I, when liberal Czechoslovakia declared independence, Mareš developed strong communist leanings and apparently had made efforts to convince Kafka and Brod of the benefits of socialism for individuals. The hardships and tragedies caused by the German occupation of his country had cemented his belief in the salvation of communist idealism—after all, the Red Army had liberated Prague. Mareš was one of many Czechs who voted Communist to bring the party to a majority in the 1946 election. And then things changed.

Observing the horrifying incidents of anti-Semitism and the violence against those with German names, Mareš became outraged at the peacetime government's blindness to the rampage and hatred. He began to report for a weekly journal, *Dnešek* (Today)—Alice emphasizes "with extraordinary bravery"—on the Czech atrocities against Jewish survivors and ethnic Germans.

In one article, "The Tragedy of the Czech Kolchoz [Cooperative Farm]," from July 11, 1946, Mareš described the destruction of the villages and damage to farms after the ethnic Germans were forced to leave. "A group of Revolutionary Guards and other gangs from the outskirts of Prague appeared in the Úštěk region and attacked the villagers with guns. . . . None of the terrified farmers had time to think of any resistance. Within two hours the action was over. Thugs have taken over a paradise that included 120 hectares of very rich land, hops fields, a wheat harvest, and over four thousand trees laden with fruits of all kinds. And today where is all that and in what condition?"

On trial in 1946 for slandering the police, Mareš spoke in

self-defense: "If there is real freedom I cannot be sentenced. If our freedom is only partial or fictitious I don't care about the sentence. . . . To keep quiet about what is happening would mean to lose one's honor. I can be silenced by force but that is the only way to keep me mute." Acquitted at his first trial, Mareš kept his promise and continued to expose the government's treatment of Czechs of German descent and all accused of German cultural sympathies. Alice admired his speaking out against injustice and the power of his pen to attract attention.

Alice and Michal Mareš began to plan a new life together in Prague. Rafi had grown attached to Mareš, and for a time it looked as if he might become part of their little family. His generosity toward Alice was nearly overwhelming. He brought her food and flowers, and one day he arrived with his most valuable possession—a small oil portrait of the head of a Parisian woman painted by Henri Toulouse-Lautrec. Though Alice won't say whether it was an engagement present, it was well known among their friends that she and Mareš were a couple. Alice was encouraged to build a new life with someone who loved her by her friend Edith Steiner-Kraus, whose husband also had not survived Auschwitz. Edith had remarried, and she and her new husband were making plans to emigrate to Palestine, because Edith believed that she would have more career opportunities in the new country.

Although the Czechs attended early discussions of the Marshall Plan, Stalin nixed their participation in the Western alliance. In early 1948, the purge of non-Communists from the ministry of the interior and the police forces intensified; the remaining twelve non-Communist members of Beneš's government resigned. In an effort to avoid civil war and greater Soviet involvement, Beneš ultimately accepted the resignations and their replacement with Communist Party members. He too resigned, on June 7, 1948.

Michal Mareš was increasingly troubled by the threat from the Soviet Union and its allies in the Czechoslovak police forces. He continued to write about the murders of Germans and the ransacking of their property, and about the involvement of Czech officials, policemen, and local dictators. He was the first to use the term *Gestapo* methods to describe the violence committed by the Czechs on the Germans in the Sudetenland, in Prague, and in various camps where the Germans were interned, awaiting their transfer to Germany. The Communist press viciously attacked Mareš, and he was expelled from the party in 1947. Shortly after the Communist takeover, in February 1948, Mareš was again arrested and this time sentenced to seven years' imprisonment on fake charges of treason. Still believing in the Czech democracy, Alice thought that he would be released quickly and their life could go on as planned.

The situation looked very different from the outside. Reading the newspaper reports, Alice's sisters in Palestine were alarmed. After Israel was proclaimed a state, on May 14, 1948, they increased their pressure on her to emigrate. As Alice continued to hold out hope for life in her homeland, Mitzi and her son, Chaim, traveled to Prague, not for a visit but to convince her twin to leave as quickly as her papers could be obtained. But when Mitzi arrived, she found Alice still optimistic about the future in Prague, and even more so about the romantic pull of a new life with Mareš.

Chaim remembers overhearing his mother and Alice talking about Mareš. "You are naïve, blind!" Mitzi insisted. "There is no future for you here."

"Mareš wants to adopt my son. We want to spend our lives together," Alice told her sister.

"Fine," Mitzi said. "He can meet you in Israel when he is out of prison."

Mitzi argued that it would be far better for Rafi to grow up among his relatives, and that Alice could have a secure life teaching at the music academy. In the end, the strength of her twin's argument won Alice over.

Alice had little time to prepare for their departure. Luck came in the acquaintance of a young Czech pilot who was flying a plane packed with Czech-manufactured arms bound for Israel. As the Communists forbade Czechs from taking anything other than their clothes out of the country, Alice needed a creative way to ship the Toulouse-Lautrec painting, Rafi's stamp collection, and her piano to Jerusalem. The pilot, who was also a musician, offered to help. Since the Communists approved of his arms cargo purchased by Israel, his flight would not be searched. During the flight, he lost power in two of his four engines, was low on fuel, and failed to make contact with the Israeli air control tower. He ditched his plane in the water. The crew survived uninjured, but the piano and the painting suffered serious damage from water and salt.

After many debilitating years, Mareš was finally released from prison because of his poor health. Although the Communists had permitted him to write weekly letters to his mother, they had neglected to inform him that she had died three years earlier. Neither he nor Alice had known at the time of Alice's emigration that travel for Czech citizens would come to be limited to trips to other Soviet Bloc countries. There would be no possibility of escape to the West or to Israel for Mareš. Had Alice stayed in Prague to be with Mareš, Rafi would have grown up without his adopted father and graduated from high school before Mareš was released from prison. Alice would have spent those years alone, and their relationship would have been unavoidably changed by the separation. And she would soon have been widowed for a second time.

Mareš spent his final years pouring his thoughts and disappointments into an unfinished autobiography that was published posthumously. He confirmed his plan to adopt Rafi, and thus his love for Alice. Alice never had the chance to explain or even say goodbye to Mareš. According to the laws, prison visitation privileges were granted only to immediate family members. And in those years communication between Alice in Israel and Mareš in a country behind the Iron Curtain was impossible. In poverty and poor health, he died in 1971. In 1991, twenty years after his death, he was fully exonerated by Václav Havel's democratic government.

Alice still thinks of him today. During one interview in December 2010, she did not talk of her husband; rather, she smiled and spoke of her admiration for the heroic Michal Mareš. "He was a brave man. Brave!" she repeated. "I had no choice. If only for Rafi's sake, in that moment I had to grab the chance to build our future in Israel. We could not wait to see what would happen. We had to leave Czechoslovakia quickly. The courage I had gained from all that had happened helped me to make that fateful decision to flee."

And as is Alice's wont, one memory leads to the next, and she closes her eyes deep in thought and speaks of Michal Mareš. "He was a kind of genius of courage. He wrote the truth. Others were too scared. Fear makes us give up. Courage gives us a chance." After a long pause she adds, "I would not be here today. Courage!"

SIX

The Tin Spoon

Alice has only good memories of her husband, who died so long ago. "He was a learned man. An extraordinary fine character. I respected him. I learned from him. He respected me . . . who I was and what music meant to me. Mutual respect is the foundation of a happy marriage."

Alice was a born romantic, just like her mother. But Sofie Herz, forsaking the man she loved, had acquiesced to her parents, who had hired a marriage broker to find the "right" husband for their daughter. That husband, Alice's father, was twenty years older than his bride-to-be and came from a country village. Friedrich Herz proved to be a worthy husband and father, although Sofie never warmed to him and always felt that she had married beneath herself intellectually because he was uneducated in literature, art, and music.

Alice was determined to make her own decisions. Perhaps she had learned from her mother's unhappiness, since Sofie had communicated clearly to her children her displeasure with her husband. As Alice grew up, she saw how her mother rarely talked with her father because, as Sofie made it known, his conversation was simply not worthwhile. Only at Friedrich's funeral did Alice learn that her father had been much loved for his generous and helpful spirit.

At the Prague Conservatory, where Alice studied piano, a tall, dashing Hungarian student, Jeno Kacliz, was obsessively attracted to Alice and her passionate playing. Ten years older and far more experienced, he tried all of his well-rehearsed seductive tricks without the anticipated success. "Music is love, and love is music," Jeno repeated endlessly. He and Alice were working on the same piece by Schumann, the C Major *Fantasy*, with the same teacher. They entered the same competitions, which Alice usually won easily. But nothing deterred Jeno from his pursuit of her. Alice finally dissuaded him, using their age difference as an excuse. During their last year together in the conservatory, she managed to keep him as a friend and colleague. Sometimes they played duets. She never heard from him again after he returned home to Hungary.

Around the same time Alice fell for the brother of her friend Trude Kraus. Unlike Jeno, Rudolf Kraus was neither tall nor good-looking; he was fifteen years older than Alice, and a dentist. She was attracted to his aura of sophistication, the way he held a cigarette and uncorked a wine bottle, even the way he would ask a simple question. Although he knew next to nothing about classical music, Rudolf had been captivated, or so he said, by a recital she had given in his family home. Alice thought Rudolf understood her, and when he took her dancing several nights each week, she felt secure in his arms. She found his flaws and failings endearing. For the first time in her life Alice was madly in love.

After several months they planned a skiing party with several friends at a hotel in the mountains. Although Alice and Rudolf took separate rooms, each had a different expectation of their holiday. Rudolf assumed that Alice's room was for appearances only; because she had agreed to spend the country holiday with him, he had taken intimacy for granted.

Alice resisted his advances. She was just getting to know him, and marriage had not been mentioned. And she had other doubts from the moment they left Prague. Rudolf seemed so different with his friends. Perhaps she did not know him at all, or the age difference was, in fact, too great. Did he truly love music, or was it a superficial interest? Maybe, like many Czech men, he had more than one girlfriend. He was, after all, a successful older man accustomed to getting his way. Instinctively Alice realized that, if he valued her, he would be patient rather than angry. On their return to the train station, the horse-drawn sleigh overturned, and while Alice was unhurt, Rudolf's hand was broken.

After their return to Prague his visits to her in her parents' home in Prague's seventh district grew less frequent. Alice thought that he might have blamed her for the accident but came to understand that he had rejected her for her sexual rebuff. Through the grapevine that was gossipy Prague at the time, Alice heard that Rudolf was seeing another woman; she knew she had been jilted. But when she learned from his sister that he was engaged, she was distraught. Knowing that he was the wrong man for her gave Alice little comfort. She told herself that Rudolf was far different from the imaginary Rudy who had conquered her heart. Yet for a time she could not bear to think of life without him.

Then, as it would throughout her life, her optimism took hold and Alice began to practice her piano without looking back. *If only* were words she banished from her vocabulary. She turned her disappointment into generosity and sent the newlyweds a small antique vase of Czech glass, with her congratulations. But the memory of her feelings for Rudolf never completely faded. Apparently his rejection deeply wounded her self-image. At 108 years of age, Alice still describes her sister Mitzi as a great beauty; "I was not at all pretty," she says. Yet in photographs, it is nearly impossible to tell the sisters apart.

Alice might never have met her future husband without another devastating loss. As a teenager she was inseparable from Trude Kraus and another friend, Daisy Klemperer.

Only twenty years old, Daisy died suddenly of an infection, which later would have been easily cured with antibiotics. It was one of the few times in her life that Alice stopped playing the piano, and her parents and friends were worried.

Several days after Daisy's funeral, Trude mentioned to Alice that a good friend in Hamburg, Leopold Sommer, had sent her a comforting letter about the tragedy. "Listen to this," Trude said as she opened the letter to read a few lines to Alice.

Leopold wrote that while the young girl's death was tragic for those who loved her, it was not so terrible for Daisy. He urged Trude and her friends to perceive the death as a warning to take the time to examine their own lives and to consider what is truly important. Cautioning against measuring the value of the individual in terms of money, public success, or other shallow standards, Leopold stressed the urgency of endeavoring to lead a purposeful life each and every day.

With those words in mind, Alice began to practice. Later she asked Trude to introduce her to Leopold.

A fine amateur violinist, Leopold Sommer had been raised in Prague, where his parents, highly educated and cultured, lived in the family's villa. Their son had elected to study business, since he felt that he was not a good enough violinist to compete in the world of professional musicians. Speaking nearly flawless English, he took his first job in the

Hamburg headquarters of a British import-export company. Several times each year he would return to Prague to visit his family. On one of these visits Trude arranged a concert in her home, with enough guests so that Leopold's introduction to Alice would not be awkward. Leopold's string quartet would perform the first half, while Alice would play after the intermission.

Leopold and Alice talked at length over tea at the end of the concert, and Leopold invited her on a date the very next day. Alice was intrigued by this knowledgeable and wise young man, whose quiet good looks she found most attractive. His visits to Prague became more frequent. Confident that his parents would approve of Alice, Leopold wasted no time arranging for Alice to play a concert in their home. The Sommers welcomed her from the start as a daughter.

When Alice's father died suddenly of a massive heart attack, Leopold rushed from Hamburg to support her at the funeral and burial. It looked as if they were destined for each other. Leopold began to seek a new position in Prague. On one of these visits, following a romantic dinner and a glorious concert, they took the steep walk up to Prague Castle. Arm in arm they looked down at their brightly lit city. Suddenly Alice announced that she wanted him to know they would get married later that year. Obviously this had been on Leopold's mind as well; he was not at all surprised at her outburst—he only asked how soon.

Alice Herz was already a successful concert pianist when she married Leopold Sommer in 1931. "He was a kind man," Alice says, and she continues to reminisce. "I was always afraid of the ways of Czech men. You know what I mean?" She is referring to the practice of married men flagrantly keeping mistresses. Alice adds, "On our wedding night I told him that I knew that I was not beautiful and that he would meet hundreds more lovely and that I would never complain. But," she says pausing, "I was lucky with my husband. He was the faithful type."

They did not indulge in a formal wedding. Rather, Alice and Leopold legalized their union privately in a civil proceeding at the Prague city hall, which was a common practice for the city's secular Jews. Alice's brother Paul was their only guest. The other family members, including her mother, stayed behind to prepare the small, celebratory family dinner that would follow their signing of the marriage contract.

Alice wore a tailored suit of periwinkle wool with white collar and trimmings. Her jacket was fashionably long; her leather high heels were ivory, as were her stockings. On her head she wore an off-white flapper-style hat. She carried a small fur muff for her white-gloved hands. The only traditional symbol of her wedding day was the bridal bouquet, of white calla lilies and roses.

Back at home, before sitting down to dine, Alice and Leopold performed Beethoven's Spring sonata for violin and piano, a fitting symbol of their union. Sofie had splurged on goose roasted with caraway seeds, wild mushrooms, fine French wine, and a cake from Prague's most expensive bakery. She was dressed in her own mother's most elegant black velvet, floor-length gown, fastened at the neck with an antique garnet brooch that Friedrich had given to her on their wedding day. As a widow and head of the house, Sofie toasted the couple. She seemed happy with her daughter's choice of husband, and she presented Alice and Leopold with money that had been saved for Alice's dowry over many years. The several thousand Czech crowns would be enough to furnish the newlyweds' apartment, which would be in the same neighborhood as Alice's mother and sister Irma. Leopold's parents honored Alice with a new Förster grand piano.

In 1937 Alice and Leopold were blessed with the birth of their son, whom they named Štěpán, after her beloved teacher. (In Israel he would change his name to the Hebrew Raphaël.) Alice practiced on her new piano and gave lessons to young students. Leopold went to the office and participated in chamber music sessions as an amateur. In the evenings they went to concerts or plays. On weekends they explored Prague's art museums and spent time with friends. Their flat was cozy. They had each other, a cook, and a nanny. But the world they knew was soon to change forever.

Hitler's troops occupied Czechoslovakia on March 15, 1939. The last known letter Leopold wrote from Prague to

Palestine in 1941 attests to the Czech Jews' efforts to live normally without complaint. He tells his brother-in-law Felix Weltsch, that, as he is writing, Alice is in the next room practicing Beethoven's Sonata no. 31 in preparation for a concert. Much of the letter includes stories about Rafi, who has turned three. "We are all well except Štěpán who has a slight cold. He talks like a waterfall and climbs on everything. He has broken two violins. We can't keep him away from the piano, which he wants to try constantly."

In 1943, when Alice and Leopold were deported to Theresienstadt, where they were forced to live separately, sometimes after work Leopold found a way to briefly visit his wife and son, and they would talk in whispers. Occasionally he was able to sneak Rafi an extra bit of bread. Rafi would be overjoyed to catch a glimpse of his father.

Alice last saw her husband on September 28, 1944, when he was shoved into a train bound for Auschwitz. "Putzi—that was his nickname," she says as she thinks of the man she had grown to love during their brief eleven years of marriage. She touches her plain wedding band, which survived the Nazis; she folds her hands and brings them close to her chest. "He was still so young."

Leopold survived Auschwitz, but as the Allies were approaching he was one of the many who were sent on to Dachau. There he died from starvation and exposure on March

28, 1945, one month and one day before Dachau was liberated, on April 29.

As a musician Alice had been trained from childhood to listen carefully when she practiced or performed. Her ability to listen to Leopold's instructions literally saved her life. During the few moments she and her husband had together before he was sent to Auschwitz, Leopold whispered, "Regardless of what the Gestapo might offer, you must never, never volunteer for anything. Never believe anything they say. Promise me this." Leopold was consumed with concern for Alice's and Rafi's survival rather than with fear of his own fate. With a final squeeze of his hand, she answered, "Yes, I promise."

Alice had to restrain six-year-old Rafi that day as he tried to run after Leopold. He told her that he wanted to take the train trip with his father. A few weeks later the Nazis offered transportation for all who wished to join their husbands. Alice heeded Leopold's advice, but many eager women and children crowded into the next transport. Neither the husbands nor their families were ever seen again.

After the war a man who had been with Leopold when he died visited Alice. He had come to bring her a small tin spoon that Leopold had used in the camps.

Today, as she sifts through a handful of mementos in a shoe box, she remembers the tin spoon and studies a photograph of her young husband. "We were good friends. We had a wonderful togetherness that could only have grown with the years. I think that Saint-Exupéry gave the best advice when he wrote, 'Love does not consist in gazing at each other, but in looking outward together in the same direction.' Everyone wants to know why I did not marry again after the war," she continues. "When it might have been possible, I was focused on earning a living and raising my child.

"Respect leads to love," Alice says. "In marriage respect is even more important than romantic love."

SEVEN

Never Too Old

Once Alice reaches a decision she rarely looks back. And so it was when the day came to leave Israel to join her son in England for a new chapter in her saga. Since both of Alice's sisters had died, Rafi argued that she was free to leave her second home. Her apartment in Jerusalem had been sold. Her bags were packed.

For some time the news of her departure had been spreading among her friends, colleagues, and students. For days she had received a constant stream of visitors who were saddened to learn that she was moving. "My last day in Jerusalem felt like an all-day open house," she recalls. "No one had been invited, but my empty apartment was filled with friends until late night. They brought food, photographs, and presents, little things they thought I would need. Israelis are so thoughtful, so giving." She comforted their tears with her smile. "Visit me in London. It is not so far away," she told them. Alice was particularly sad to leave her closest friend, the pianist Edith Steiner-Kraus. They had sustained each other throughout their imprisonment in Theresienstadt and shared the joys of their new life in the nascent Israeli nation. Edith asked, "Will I ever see you again? Do you remember that first time I rang your doorbell in Prague and asked if you would hear me play the Smetana dances?" Alice added, "You were a magnificent pianist. I was so impressed. You instinctively felt the Czech rhythms. We will always be friends." That final evening they promised to telephone each other every week.

Mitzi's only child, Chaim Adler—who had met Alice at the dock when she arrived in Israel by boat in 1949—drove her to the airport in Tel Aviv. When the time came to board the flight, Alice and her nephew embraced. In that moment, a half century of memories passed unspoken between them. Then Alice walked resolutely toward the departure gate.

Raphaël had settled permanently in London with his wife, Sylvie Ott, and their two small sons, David and Ariel, combining his concert career with the security of a teaching position in Manchester. Some years after his marriage ended amicably in 1978, he fell in love with Geneviève Teulières, a French woman he had known decades earlier when they were fellow students in Paris. When Rafi became a professor of cello at Guildhall School of Music in London he gave up his commute to Manchester to spend more time at home.

Recognizing his mother's advanced age, Rafi and Geneviève encouraged Alice to retire from teaching and move to London. Alice had learned rudimentary English as a child, and she had practiced it whenever possible and especially on her visits to England, which had been getting longer over the years; perfecting the language did not present the same challenges she had faced with learning Hebrew. Alice loved the vibrant musical life in London, the massive trees and sprawling ivy everywhere, and the way "everything is available." But while she enjoyed the cooler English summers, her son was the only reason she made so many trips.

When Rafi asked his mother to move permanently to London to be near him, she was, at first, resistant to the idea. Retirement was an unfamiliar concept to Alice. She could not imagine life without work. "Why should I stop teaching?" she asked. Alice was perfectly healthy and felt that she was needed by her Israeli students. "I love my students and they love me," she told her son. It even felt ungrateful to Alice to leave the country that had given her the chance to rebuild her life. And it was the nation that had educated her son, the land he had served for two years in the military. Rafi was exempt from national service because he was a Holocaust survivor and an only child. Yet he and Alice agreed that he should give back to the nation that had welcomed them when they were stateless. Alice was proud of Rafi for playing cello in the army orchestra and saxophone in the band.

Alice would be leaving nephews and nieces and their children behind. She would have to face all of the endless details that make life work, from finding a new doctor and pharmacy and trying a different diet to learning her way around the city and all its cultural activities. But after she had made the decision to immigrate, her optimism took over and she proceeded determinedly to make plans for the next phase of her life. The apartment she had purchased in London was a one-room pied-à-terre and not nearly large enough for her precious Steinway grand piano. She had no choice but to sell the instrument and to give away most of her furniture. As the date of her departure approached, the process became more automatic and less emotional. After all, Alice had never been attached to material possessions. In the end she shipped her upright piano, photographs, and other small mementos to her new home, arriving in England with little more than the clothes on her back, and settling into a space less than half the size of her comfortable flat in Jerusalem.

From her first days in London's Hampstead section Alice established a routine that would help to keep her physically strong. She began her day with a walk to a swimming pool where she would exercise for an hour. Since childhood she had been a strong swimmer, and she was accustomed to walking everywhere in Jerusalem in the same way that she had explored Prague on foot. When she returned home Alice would practice the piano for at least three hours, which always sustained her spirits. During the first few months, as word spread in the Czech and Israeli émigré communities that Alice was living in London, a handful of students found their way to her door. Without losing time she began to attend concerts and make new and lasting friends. Alice was anxious to reestablish her independence despite the fact that she had moved to be near her son and her grandchildren.

In 1986, not long after her move to England, eighty-three-year-old Alice was diagnosed with breast cancer. Rafi went with his mother to the doctor's appointment, where they explored her treatment options. The concerned surgeon, not wanting to alarm her, explained in great detail that breast cancer in an older woman did not carry the same implications it did for those much younger. "We can do surgery—that is, we can remove your breast. But your recovery will take some time, and because of your advanced age, the risks from the anesthesia and the surgery itself are more significant."

"What will happen if you do not do surgery?" Alice asked.

"Well, at your age," the doctor began again, "the tumors

grow more slowly. The chances of your living long enough to suffer the most severe effects of this cancer are very low."

With that answer, Alice gave Rafi her most insulted look before responding with "In this case I want the surgery. How soon can it be done? Cancers must be removed."

Rafi chimed in, "Doctor, my mother is otherwise healthy. She swims at least one mile daily and eats a healthy diet. Do not think of her as old."

Laughing, she says, "It is twenty-five years later and I am still here. My son was right."

Alice's piano playing, her great good humor, and her interest in nearly everything from literature to the lives of elephants and philosophy touched Valerie Reuben, a former publishing executive who lives in the same apartment house as Alice. Increasingly intrigued with the elderly pianist, Mrs. Reuben suggested that Alice attend classes with her at the University of the Third Age.

Founded at Cambridge University by social entrepreneurs, the University of the Third Age is a university in the ancient and original sense of a group that gathers for the stated purpose of study. Alice's most inspiring teacher there is Ralph Blumenau, the author of *Philosophy and Living*. According to Blumenau, the university "is not actually a university in the normal sense, in that it has no examinations and awards no qualifications, but exists for retired people who wish to keep their minds active." The largest division of the university, near Alice's home, boasts more than 140 courses and fifteen thousand members. The teachers are all volunteers, and some classes run themselves, with the students leading the research and giving lectures; yet the course work is hardly less stringent than if one were studying for a degree.

Alice seized the opportunity and immediately enrolled in two classes: one on modern European history and the other on the works of Spinoza and Kant. It did not take long for her fellow students and the professors to see that Alice was unlike most of the other students. She would read and reread the assigned texts and boldly ask piercing questions, challenging the professors at each session. On the topic of historical study, she brought up the issue of accuracy and reliable interpretation. "How do you know when a historian is prejudiced and presents the facts in a twisted way to prove his premise?" Alice asked. And more than once she engaged in a discussion of which discipline should be studied first, history or philosophy. Alice had found, as a lay student, that she understood philosophy most clearly when it was presented against the historical times of the philosopher or through some decisive life experience.

Alice's interest in philosophy had been sparked when her brother-in-law Felix Weltsch introduced her to the subject while he was studying for his Ph.D. at Charles University.

But it was not until she began to study philosophy formally at the University of the Third Age that she was able to delve into the works of Spinoza. Professor Blumenau had impressed her with his extraordinary book, which explained the way ancient philosophers influence our ethics and our attitudes toward life and the world around us.

After Rafi's untimely death in 2001, Alice turned to the search for meaning in her life more passionately than ever. How could she explain all she had seen? How could she continue to live with and beyond her greatest tragedy? Reading Spinoza, she gained insight into the events of her own life. Though the philosopher died more than two hundred years before Alice was born, his thoughts struck her as applicable to her own time, and they resonated with her beliefs. A natural existentialist, Alice had always felt that no one is all good or all evil, and that it is up to the individual to cope with both sides of his or her nature. Alice herself tried to concentrate on the best in every situation she faced. Spinoza argued that God and Nature are synonymous and that, just as God and Nature are infinite, both good and evil are part of what we call existence. He believed that everything is connected to everything else; that we must love God, but that God does not necessarily love us; and that a life of reason and knowledge is the highest virtue. For Spinoza, Existence is God.

Alice accepts Spinoza's explanation of the concept of God. Although he was accused of being an atheist, Spinoza was a deeply spiritual person who loved the infinite God. Based on his philosophy, Spinoza became a prophet of democratic values, separation of church and state, and tolerance among nations and people. The American forefathers who drafted the Constitution of the United States in the eighteenth century were profoundly influenced by Spinoza's modern ideas. And breaking with the very strict Portuguese-Spanish orthodox beliefs of his youth, Baruch Spinoza pleaded for authentic faith rather than a dogmatic or gullible religion.

Alice looked to Arthur Schopenhauer and Friedrich Nietzsche for their thoughts on music. She never tires of quoting both of them from memory. Alice reminds those who might not take the time to go to a concert or pay for their child's music lessons that Nietzsche wrote, "Without music life would be a mistake." Although Alice loves poetry and painting and architecture, she agrees with Schopenhauer that music is the highest of all the arts.

Alice continued to attend classes three times each week at the university until she was 104 years old. She is a strong believer in formal learning as a major factor in longevity, in keeping our minds as well as our bodies active and positive. And although today Alice no longer leaves her home to attend classes, her beloved Professor Blumenau has become so committed to Alice that he visits her at least once each semester for an afternoon of philosophical discussion.

INTERLUDE

Chicken Soup

Around twenty-five years ago, Alice established disciplined eating habits that have not varied. In order to conserve her most precious and finite commodity, time, as well as for health reasons, she decided to eat the same meals each day. This would preclude wasting valuable moments trying to decide what to cook or eat. She could save time because her weekly shopping list would never vary. After she had cooked for the week, ten minutes to reheat and eat the food was the limit. Beyond that, she felt, the meal was not worthwhile.

Alice feels no nostalgia for the complicated and lavish cream-laden dishes from her childhood under the Hapsburg Empire. She rejects them outright and opts for healthy simplicity. Having decided that caffeine is harmful for her, she has eliminated all tea and coffee, as well as wine or any form of alcohol. She begins her daily regimen with a slice of toast topped with a piece of feta cheese. Half a banana or an apple and a cup of hot water complete her first meal of the day. For lunch and dinner she eats a bowl of chicken soup.

Alice sips hot water throughout the day and occasionally snacks on fruit. On most days, however, she eats nothing else—unless a visitor brings chocolates, a home-baked cake, or a lemon meringue pie, all of which she enjoys immensely. Although Alice has accrued disciplined life habits, she has never been rigid. "I am very independent" has been one of her mantras, and the diet she devised for herself was one that she could prepare alone well into her 105th year. Because of her failing vision and sometimes unsteady walk, Alice has finally agreed to substitute her lunch of chicken soup for meals on wheels. Still, at age 108 she manages her own breakfast and supper of toast and cheese and leftovers from lunch. Of course she misses her chicken soup, but she is enthusiastic about the hot midday meal of some kind of meat or chicken and two small servings of vegetables, which arrives promptly at one in the afternoon in its small black plastic container. Most of all she enjoys welcoming the smiling faces of the young delivery men or women, who greet her by name. Observing her eagerly opening and relishing the unappetizing-looking contents of the package, her friend Anita teases her, saying, "You are the only person in the world who loves that food." "It tastes good to me, I am hungry," Alice counters as she ravenously digs in. Yet the occasional gift from a thoughtful neighbor or friend of homemade chicken soup continues to be the nectar of the gods for Alice.

Until she was past ninety, Alice baked a luscious apple cake for her guests. The recipe she learned from her mother had been handed down from her Moravian grandmother. Central Europeans have always been fond of dense cakes made with nuts and fruit that can be eaten at any time of the day. Alice often served it to her guests at teatime.

CHICKEN SOUP

Ingredients

2 large onions, coarsely chopped
2 large garlic cloves, chopped
5 stalks celery, cut into 3-inch pieces
8 carrots, sliced
½ green pepper, chopped
2 parsnips, chopped
1 small tomato, chopped
¼ cup fresh parsley
1 cup fresh dill
1 Knorr chicken broth cube
6 whole cloves
One 3–4 lb. chicken, cut in half
3 leeks (white part only)
7 shallots, left whole but peeled
1 tablespoon salt

½ teaspoon ground black pepper
Sprigs of dill, for garnish

Add the onion, garlic, celery, carrots, green pepper, parsnip, tomato, parsley, dill, chicken broth cube, and cloves to a soup pot filled with 2½ quarts cold water. Bring to a boil, cover, and simmer over low heat for ½ hour. Add the chicken, and salt and pepper to taste. Bring to a boil, cover, and simmer on top of the stove for ½ hour. Add the leeks and shallots, bring to a boil, cover, and simmer for 1 hour. Taste for salt and pepper. When the soup is cool, remove the chicken, discard the skin and bones. Replace the chicken slices into the soup. Degrease the soup. (I chill the soup in the refrigerator to be able to skim all fat from the broth.) Reheat, garnish with dill, and serve with warm French or Italian bread. Serves 4 as an entrée.

ALICE'S APPLE CAKE

Ingredients

2 cups all-purpose flour
2 teaspoons baking powder
1 teaspoon baking soda
¾ teaspoon ground allspice
2 teaspoons finely ground cinnamon
1 teaspoon finely ground nutmeg
½ teaspoon ground cloves
1 cup light brown sugar, packed
1 cup granulated white sugar
3 large whole eggs

1 teaspoon pure vanilla extract

2 sticks (16 ounces) unsalted butter, softened

4 Granny Smith or Golden Delicious apples, peeled, cored, and coarsely chopped

3 tablespoons Calvados (optional)

1 cup walnuts, coarsely chopped

¾ cup raisins

2 tablespoons confectioners' sugar

Preheat oven to 350 degrees Fahrenheit.

Butter a bundt or angel food cake pan well and dust with flour, making certain that the bottom and sides of the pan are covered to prevent sticking. Discard the excess flour.

Sift together the flour, baking powder and soda, allspice, cinnamon, nutmeg, and cloves. Add the brown and granulated white sugars to the mixture. Add the eggs, vanilla, and softened butter. Beat with electric beaters for about 4 minutes or until the batter is very smooth.

Peel and coarsely chop the apples and chop the nuts. Add the optional Calvados to the chopped apples and stir well several times. Discard any liquid that accumulates in the bottom of the bowl. Add the apples, nuts, and raisins to the cake mixture. Pour into the baking pan and place in the center of the preheated oven. Bake for 1 hour. When the cake is done, it will shrink from the sides of the pan. Remove from the baking pan and place on a serving platter to cool. Before serving sift 1 or 2 tablespoons of confectioners' sugar on the top.

EIGHT

Music Was Our Food

On Alice's third day in Theresienstadt, she was told to play a recital the following week. "But I need to practice," she responded.

"Can you imagine," Alice says today, "they said I would be allowed to rehearse only one hour each day before I went to my assigned work?" Alice's first job was in the laundry. Eventually she was ordered to split mica chips for war production—hard and dangerous work for a pianist's hands.

The next morning Alice found the room where she had been assigned the 9:00–10:00 A.M. practice slot. With no time to waste she began to practice her Chopin études, only to find that the pedal did not work and several keys stuck repeatedly. Refusing to be defeated, she quickly adapted to the piano's limitations and began to play with abandon, losing herself in the music. "At least I was making music and that always made me happy," she says when she considers the circumstances. Practicing with her eyes closed, she was so engrossed in the melody of the étude in A-flat Major that she did not hear the door open or footsteps crossing the floor. When Alice paused for a moment, a familiar voice said, "Very impressive, Alice, and on that broken-down old piano." It was Hans Krása, a handsome, bon vivant composer whom Alice had known in Prague. In the months since they had last met, he had become older and thinner. "I'm so glad you are still here. Are you all right?" Alice was unable to hide her tears. Everywhere, every day, since she had arrived in Theresienstadt, she had been searching for her mother, asking everyone if they had seen her, even though Alice knew the awful truth. Krása had known her mother and recognized Alice as a major pianist. Though he had no answers for her, Krása responded with Czech humor. "Well, I must apologize that I cannot invite you to my castle. But may I listen to you practice?"

On June 10, 1940, the Gestapo took control of Terezín, a small town one hour's drive from Prague, immediately turning the immense brick-walled eighteenth-century garrison town into a ghetto and the adjacent smaller fort into their prison for political enemies. By the end of that year they had forced all the Czech residents of the town to evacuate their homes and had dispatched a shipment of young and strong

Jewish men to transform the buildings into a concentration camp.

Identified by its German name, Theresienstadt, it was conceived by Hitler as a "model" camp and officially established on November 24, 1941. Cunningly organized by Reinhard Heydrich and Adolf Eichmann to deflect and hide the truth of the Nazis' mass murders of Europe's Jews, it was advertised as a spa town, where Jews could be resettled to comfortably live out the war. As part of the ruse, it was the only camp where Jews could apply for admission and special privileges, and pay their own travel expenses; they could even—for a very high price—request a view of either a peaceful lake or a beautiful mountain from their new home. These were just added ploys for the Nazis to confiscate people's money, jewels, and property before killing them.

Still living in Prague, Alice and Leopold began to hear the rumors of death, diseases, lack of sanitation, and contaminated water there. And after the first transports of human cargo from Theresienstadt to the East, the truth behind the rumors began to emerge: in place of pleasant apartments, Czechoslovak Jewish citizens—including musicians, writers, scientists, and teachers—were being herded together into airless rooms without privacy, sanitary facilities, or food. Theresienstadt was both a ghetto and a concentration camp.

Most of the prisoners were crowded into either large

military barracks or the small houses that the former citizens of the town had built to shelter single families. Some of the new arrivals were crammed into larger buildings that had once been offices or schools. One of the biggest problems in the beginning was the lack of toilets. People waited in long lines, and toilet paper was forbidden for Jews. Not even sick children or the elderly were allowed to go to the front of the line.

So many of the Jews whom the Prague Jewish Council—under the strict supervision of Nazi officers—had sent to Theresienstadt were musicians, artists, and writers that, as soon as they arrived in Theresienstadt, they began organizing musical activities secretly, in spite of the fact that any type of music making had initially been strictly prohibited. Many of the musicians had cleverly smuggled their instruments into the camp. In order to hide his cello one artist completely dismantled it, buried the parts in his clothes, and then glued the pieces together again in a men's barrack. Although the artists were careful to stage their improvised concerts clandestinely in basements or attics, they would be discovered. To their surprise, however, the artists were not met with punishment but ordered to perform more frequently.

The Nazis understood that adding musical and artistic events to their spa setting could be a huge publicity stunt to prove to the outside world that all was well with the Jews.

Thus they ordered the prisoners to form a *Freizeitgestaltung,* or Free Time Committee, to organize concerts, lectures, and other events. Hans Krása was named head of the musical section. Crudely printed posters appeared in barracks to advertise the programs. Because of the overwhelming response, tickets—free, because prisoners had no money—were distributed to control admittance. Even music critics were encouraged to write reviews. So many musicians were among the prisoners sent to Theresienstadt that for a short time four symphony orchestras could play simultaneously. Theresienstadt was the only place in occupied Europe where jazz was performed—the Nazis called it "degenerate music" and had banned it not only because it was American but also because it was played by blacks and Jews.

The artists took their performances just as seriously as if they were on the world stage. Not only were they trying to inspire their prisoner audiences but the musicians were playing for one another. Alice says, "As our situation became more difficult, we tried even harder to reach for perfection, for the meaning in the music. Music was our way of remembering our inner selves, our values."

After the war Edith Steiner-Kraus was offended when questioned about the quality of the performances in Theresienstadt. "You are no doubt speaking about precise rhythm, intonation, balance, diction. . . . The superficial nature of your question troubles me terribly—as if any of that mattered. Don't you understand? We had returned to the source of the music. . . . I don't understand why people, when they talk about Theresienstadt, mention those elements that you ask about. You'll never understand, or get close, to what music truly meant to each of us as a sustaining power and as a way of using our skills to inspire, beyond criticism, beyond any superficial evaluation. We *were* music."

While performing, the prisoners could nearly forget their hunger and their surroundings. Besides the terror of finding their names on a deportation list to the East, the fear of dying of starvation, typhus, and other diseases had become a reality. Medicine was forbidden for Jews. Hundreds of bodies were carted off daily. Between those who were sent on to Auschwitz and other death camps in the East, and those who would perish from illness, of the more than 156,000 who passed through those gates, only 11 percent would survive until liberation, on May 8, 1945.

The novelist Ivan Klíma wrote after the war of his first night in Theresienstadt "as a boy of thirteen," sitting alone among many elderly, sick people and watching a performance of Smetana's opera *The Bartered Bride*. "There were no costumes, no orchestra, no set; it was cold, but we sat transfixed by the music. Many cried. I felt like crying too. Years later when I saw a beautifully produced performance it was not nearly so moving as I had remembered."

What the Nazis failed to understand was that the power

of music to provide comfort and hope to the performers and their audiences was stronger than the terror of their masters. Every composition that was written in Theresienstadt, and every concert played there, became a moral victory against the enemy. The beauty of their civilization became for many prisoners a shield against despair. Through music, the performers could hold on to their personal identities, while the audiences, transported out of time and place through the music, could for the duration of the performances feel that life was almost normal.

Before the deportations, since the Nazis had banned performances by Jews, concerts in Prague were moved to undisclosed venues. By late 1939 the Prague Jewish Orphanage had become one such location. The theater could seat nearly 150 people, but it was dangerous for so many to be noticed coming or leaving, even in darkness. Most of the audience would sleep on the floor to avoid arrest. The atmosphere at the concerts was in complete contrast to the daily reality of restrictions, humiliations, ever-changing ordinances, and arrests. Alice gave several full-length recitals at the orphanage. "My audiences wanted to hear Beethoven, Schubert, Czech composers, and the music of Mendelssohn that the Nazis banned. We did not listen to them, we chose not to hear. Can you imagine," she asks, "that Hitler tried to destroy all memories of Mendelssohn, who only one century before had been recognized as a German hero—and all because he was born Jewish?" Mendelssohn, who was raised as a Lutheran convert, wrote works based on Christian texts. "What could they have been thinking when the brownshirts burned his music, obliterated the statue of him, and destroyed portraits of him right in front of the Leipzig Gewandhaus while Sir Thomas Beecham was conducting a concert that night of November 10, 1936? People still said, it can't get worse. Hitler's regime is an aberration. The question we should have been asking was, if this is what the Nazis did to the dead, what would happen to living Jews?"

At the request of Rudi Freudenfeld, the son of the orphanage's director, Alice presented a few programs for the young audience. Rudi, a teacher, had volunteered to help with the many children sent to Prague from Poland and other countries farther east by parents who had mistakenly hoped that they would be safe there. Now that Jewish children were forbidden all education—public and private—they had little to occupy their time.

In 1938, Hans Krása composed a short opera based on a fairy tale invented by his friend Adolf Hoffmeister, which had never been performed. They had titled their one-act opera *Brundibár* ("little bee" in Czech), after the name of the main character. Since for inexplicable reasons the Nazis had not restricted artistic activities for children, Krása and Hoffmeister offered to help occupy the youngsters' time with a

production of their opera. Building the sets, making costumes, learning their roles, participating in rehearsals and
performances could provide distraction for the children,
who were not allowed to play outside. Preparations soon
began, with the goal of a performance to be staged in the
orphanage. Their one full rehearsal took place for a small
audience in early 1942. And then the Nazis began to deport
the children—along with their teachers, Krása, Hoffmeister,
and Freudenfeld—to the newly established concentration
camp at Theresienstadt.

During her first months in Theresienstadt, Alice was
able to play chamber music concerts, but most of the string
players were quickly transported to Auschwitz. In a strange
way, despite the filth and hunger, her routine life of working an obligatory factory job, performing, caring for Rafi,
and giving him and a few other children elementary piano
lessons whenever she had a spare moment helped her never
to lose hope. Meanwhile, Hans Krása decided to try to stage
Brundibár again as a way of occupying and entertaining
some of the thousands of children. Rudi Freudenfeld had
smuggled his copy of the score with piano accompaniment
into the camp, and Krása reorchestrated the opera for the
thirteen available instrumentalists. A most unconventional
ensemble, it included violin, cello, piano, accordion, and
trumpet played by a mixture of old and young musicians.
A ten-year-old boy from Denmark was chosen to play the

trumpet part, an exceptionally difficult piece for his age. Freudenfeld taught the music to the children and conducted the performances.

Alice thought that Rafi might enjoy participating in the performance and asked Krása to arrange an audition for him. With his clear voice, perfect pitch, and excellent Czech diction, Rafi was given the small solo role of the sparrow, although at age seven he would be the youngest member of the cast.

Brundibár is a kind of moral fairy tale where good triumphs over evil. Two characters, Pepiček and Aninka, have a very sick mother. The doctor prescribes milk for her with the warning that without the milk she will soon die. But there is no money to buy it. Seeing the organ grinder Brundibár as he plays on the street corner, the children begin singing, hoping the villagers will throw coins to them. But the cruel Brundibár chases them away. Three animals— a dog, cat, and sparrow—come to their aid. Together with the neighborhood children, they sing a lullaby. People are impressed and reward them with coins, which Brundibár immediately steals from them. All the children and animals chase him and recover their bag of money. The opera ends with the children singing a marchlike song of victory over the evil Brundibár, a stand-in for Hitler.

The audience reveled in the opera's allegorical protest. Since the Nazis had dictated that operas must be presented only in German, it is astonishing that they ignored the fact that all fifty-five performances of *Brundibár* were sung in Czech right under their noses. Most likely the Nazis did not trouble themselves to translate the libretto because they attached no significance to a work performed by Jewish children. Ironically the Nazis capitalized on the little opera for their own propaganda, featuring it in a performance for the Swiss Red Cross. In the 1944 propaganda film *The Führer Gives the Jews a City,* Rafi can be seen singing in the front row on the far left of the screen, standing on a box because he was the smallest member of the cast. Rafi loved being onstage. He would sometimes say, "When I grow up, I will be an actor." Alice did not fail to notice that her son and the other children who performed in *Brundibár* were immensely strengthened by the experience. "When they were singing and acting the children could enter into the magic of theater and pretend they were back at home. They could ignore for a moment or two their hunger and fear," she says.

Today *Brundibár* is the only world-class opera composed for performance by children. It is produced continually by opera companies and schools around the world.

Over time the prisoners discovered somewhat better pianos in the basements of the houses and warehouses and carried them into several of the larger rooms in the former city hall and the Magdeburg Barracks, where *Brundibár* was initially performed. And occasionally, when the camp was expecting a visit from an important person, the Nazis supplied something better from their storehouse of confiscated Jewish instruments. A gifted prisoner would do his best to tune and repair the pianos. By mid-1944 Alice's allotted practice time was increased to two hours daily so that she could give more concerts. When she accompanied a soloist, Rafi would often turn the pages. He was so alert and accurate that he became a regular page turner for other artists as well.

Between the summer of 1943 and liberation, Alice played more than one hundred concerts, mostly solo recitals culled from memory from her extensive repertoire. When they first arrived at the camp, Leopold and Rafi usually sat together in the first row during her performances. Most often her program would include a Beethoven sonata, works by Chopin or Schumann, and several pieces by Czech composers. Viktor Ullmann and others would review Alice's concerts. When he arrived in Theresienstadt, Ullmann was assigned to work for the *Freizeitgestaltung* (Free Time Organization) as a music critic and was also given the job of scheduling the pianists' practice times. At concerts he could be seen scribbling in pencil on paper. Ullmann was allowed to type his essays in the Freizeitgestaltung's office, where a few copies would be made for distribution to the artists. Before his deportation to Auschwitz, in 1944, he penned a tribute to thank Alice "for the many beautiful hours" she gave to all who listened. This article was discovered in a collection of twenty-seven of Ullmann's reviews after the war.

Several times Alice performed all of the twenty-four Chopin études, a daunting task under the best circumstances. Another reviewer named her "Chopin's Divine Mirror" and wrote, "Only one interpreter can make immortal in innate perfection the melancholy and sweetness of the young Chopin . . . the artist Mrs. Herz Sommer." Anna Flachová, who was a young girl in the camp, credits Alice's performance there with inspiring her to become a musician. After the war she studied piano and voice, and today she is a vocal coach in the conservatory in Brno.

"We were not competitive," Alice explains. "We did our best to support and encourage each other and to dream together for our future. Sometime in 1944 a new pianist arrived who wanted to play Bach's Italian Concerto in one of our joint concerts. Music scores were, of course, forbidden, and she did not have the piece memorized. Edith offered her help. She wrote out the entire piece by hand—all three movements—from memory." Alice adds her favorite word of praise, "Extraordinary." She smiles recalling Pavel Haas's *Three Chinese Songs,* which he composed in the camp for the bass singer Karel Berman. "Haas was ingenious to write music on Chinese love poetry in a concentration camp." The songs were such a success that after the war Berman would frequently be asked to sing them in memory of Haas in Prague.

Alice accompanied some of the rehearsals and thinks that she played for one or two of the performances of Verdi's Requiem, which the conductor Rafael Schächter was preparing for the upcoming visit by the International Red Cross hosted by Adolf Eichmann. By mid-1944 not enough orchestra players were left to make up the large symphony required for the requiem—they had already been transported to Auschwitz. "Schächter had to conduct the requiem with only piano accompaniment—very difficult music for the pianist," Alice explains. The conductor had managed to smuggle only one copy of the score into the camp, so he taught the singers the music and words by rote, and everyone sang the entire requiem from memory. And Schächter had to train a new choir at least three times, as the numbers were decimated by the deportations to Auschwitz. Alice never fails to mention that her friend Karel Berman sang the bass solos for all fifteen performances.

Some prisoners criticized Schächter for choosing a piece based on Christian text rather than a Jewish liturgical work, and many of the Czechs thought that he should have performed a work by a Czech composer. "Schächter and his singers felt strongly about the Verdi because it was modern and universal," Alice says. Schächter's final "command" performance was staged by the Nazis for the representatives of the International Red Cross on June 23, 1944.

On October 28 the last transport, with a cargo of two thousand Jews, left from Theresienstadt bound for Auschwitz. It arrived in time for most of its passengers to be processed into the gas chambers on October 30. On orders from Himmler, the gas chambers were then shut down. Bitterly aware that they were losing the war, he was anxious to destroy the evidence. By November 1944, most of Alice's friends and colleagues—including the assistant concertmaster of the Czech Philharmonic, the kindly Egon Ledeč, the conductor Rafael Schächter, and the composers Pavel Haas, Viktor Ullmann, Hans Krása, and Gideon Klein—had perished. Alice and her friend Edith Steiner-Kraus were the only two prominent pianists left in the camp. During the last few months of the war, Czech Jews who had previously been exempted because they were married to Aryans were deported to Theresienstadt. Alice's brother Paul arrived in that group with his violin. As when they were children, Alice and Paul played recitals of Beethoven's sonatas for violin and piano.

Alice believes that, despite the conditions in the camp and the inadequate, broken-down, legless instruments provided for concerts, emotionally she may have given her finest interpretations of Beethoven's and Schubert's sonatas in Theresienstadt. The music in her mind and under her fingers was her only possession. Proudly and carefully she prepared each program so that her audience of prisoners could experience the splendor and richness of life that was denied to them in the camp. "We were not heroic," Alice says. "We improvised. We managed to keep doing, keep working as usual. To not practice was unthinkable."

In that bizarre make-do concert hall, Alice played for some of the most distinguished audiences of her life. Clinging to their own humanity, Alice's close friend Rabbi Leo Baeck and his friend and colleague Dr. Viktor Frankl were always seated near the stage. People who otherwise would have heard her performances only in the great concert halls of Europe gratefully sat crowded with children and ordinary citizens, including Henry Kissinger's aunt Minna, Sigmund Freud's sister Adolfine, Franz Kafka's sister Ottla, and nearly the entire Czech musical establishment.

As Alice says, "Music was our food. This I can say. When we have something spiritual, maybe we don't need food. Music was life. We did not, could not, would not give up."

NINE

The Führer Gives the Jews a City

Alice shakes her head as she recalls the spring of 1944. "The Nazis announced what they called the Theresienstadt 'beautification project' in preparation for the inspection tour of the Red Cross on June 23. They told us that we would all need to work harder to be proud of our city. We [prisoners] laughed. We knew that it was a trick."

The International Red Cross had been pressuring the Nazis to allow an inspection of Theresienstadt for some time. They had been tipped off to the fact that the prisoners were not as well treated as reported by the Germans. The Nazis finally agreed to a visit by three representatives, one from the Danish Red Cross and two from the Swiss Red Cross. It was to be tightly controlled; the representatives would not be free to wander about or to talk directly to prisoners. The SS would escort their guests at all times, showing them only preselected, specially prepared buildings and re-hearsed scenes.

Although the German Army was retreating on all fronts, the secret war on the Jews was being sped up. The designers of the Final Solution were dedicated to finishing what they had started—the total destruction of the Jews. Still, the Nazi high command, anxious to protect their own skins, wanted to deceive the West about their intentions regarding their "Jewish problem." The Nazis thought that they could surely dupe the Red Cross during their one-day "spa" visit but felt they needed a still grander propaganda campaign. Concurrent with the prisoners' hard labor on the "beautification" project, the Nazis discovered their propaganda weapon in Kurt Gerron, one of Germany's most famous actors and screen directors. And, of course, they gave their word of honor to Gerron, a Jew, that he and his wife would not be sent to Auschwitz.

Gerron played a major role in Bertolt Brecht's *Three-penny Opera* with his indelible delivery of the opening song, "Mack the Knife," at the premiere in Berlin in 1928. He became a film star after his role as Kiepert, the magician, in Germany's first major sound film, *The Blue Angel* with Marlene Dietrich. Already incarcerated in Theresienstadt, he was ordered to make a film depicting the Nazi lies of the "beautiful life" that the Führer provided for the Jews in the spa town. SS officers were on the set at all times, barking orders to Gerron. They wanted a scene of Jews laughing at a theatrical performance. But the prisoners would not, could not, laugh. As the SS pressure increased, a terrified, sweating Gerron begged his prisoner-actors to laugh on command for the camera. Relying on his directorial instincts, Gerron began to wobble his fat belly in such a way that he elicited uproarious laughter for a few rare moments. Later Kurt Gerron would bear the dubious distinction of directing the only known film made inside an operational concentration camp.

While he prepared to shoot, all aspects of the Nazi hoax rapidly progressed. Jewish slave labor was forced to paint the interiors and exteriors of the buildings that would be showcased. In order to avoid the appearance of overcrowding, the Gestapo rushed 7,503 older and sick prisoners to their deaths in Auschwitz between May 16 and May 18, 1944. The third bunks were temporarily removed from the beds in one of the women's buildings. Curtains were added to the windows, and books were strewn about temporary tables to create a homey environment. Trees and flowers were planted, street and building signs with German names were erected. Even a bank was opened that distributed fake and worthless Theresienstadt bills. Suddenly there was a Main Street with a beauty shop and café, a bakery and a coffee shop stocked with spectacular goods, including mouthwatering petits fours and a tiered wedding cake that the starving prisoners were forbidden to touch. The streets the Red Cross officials would walk had been scrubbed with brushes, soap, and water by prisoners on their hands and knees. But all was a sham, a fake movie set, which would be destroyed as soon as the film was completed and the representatives of the Red Cross had departed.

As word of the Nazi propaganda film spread throughout the camp, many prisoners advised Gerron to refuse to cooperate. Although he did protest, he hoped that making the film would put off his deportation to Auschwitz, and he hoped that his carefully crafted images would be able to convey the truth behind the sham. In addition, his depressed mood improved when he found himself working once again in his profession. He immediately wrote a script. His original storyboards, approved by the Nazis, were discovered in Theresienstadt after the war.

Gerron insisted on hiring one of Czechoslovakia's finest cameramen, Ivan Frič, and his crew from Prague. The Nazis complied, although they probably feared that the truth of their enterprise would be endangered by civilian Czech exposure to the camp. The director, however, countered that he needed the experienced crew in order to make the film they wanted.

All of the more than thirty thousand prisoners left in Theresienstadt were affected by the production of the film. Many who appeared even fleetingly in the film wrongly believed that by cooperating they would be saved. Prisoners were assigned work as makeup artists and hairdressers. Most of the prisoners, including those who were simply members of the audience at concerts or a soccer game, were given costumes culled from the extensive Nazi warehouses of the confiscated belongings of the dead. But dress shoes for the orchestra were in short supply; so many shoes had been sent to Greater Germany to be given to civilians who had lost everything in bombing raids that not enough pairs in diverse sizes were available. Gerron solved that problem by placing flowerpots around the edge of the stage, hiding the players' feet.

Although most of the film was shot in Theresienstadt between August and September, it appears that Gerron either filmed part of the Red Cross visit in June or inserted available Nazi footage taken that day. His film includes the carefully rehearsed act of a Jewish boy running into the street after a ball. A uniformed Nazi catches the ball and gives it to the child with a friendly pat on his head. A few weeks later, that same child was murdered in Auschwitz.

While the representative of the Danish Red Cross was not deluded by the charade, the Swiss delegation accepted it. The Swiss issued their report concurring with the Nazis that the Jews were relatively well off compared with German civilians who lived in bombed-out cities.

The king of Denmark, Christian X, reacted differently.

He demanded that the 466 Danish Jews of Theresienstadt be released and safely returned to Denmark. The Nazis acquiesced, and a convoy of white buses and ambulances crossed front lines to try to rescue all of the Danish prisoners. But it was too late for the fifty Danes who had already died in the camp. Paul Sanford, the twelve-year-old Danish orphan who had played the trumpet part in the orchestra accompanying the performances of *Brundibár*, was one of the prisoners saved by his nation's successful intervention.

Even after the Red Cross officials had departed, through the summer of 1944 and until the end of the filming, Gerron walked a tenuous line, trying to satisfy the Nazis' demands and at the same time to expose the truth. Regardless of the background or the scenes of a well-dressed population, with close-up shots Gerron was able to depict the depressed, lifeless faces around him. As an audience listened to *Study for Strings*, which Pavel Haas had written for the occasion and which was conducted by Karel Ančerl, who survived to become the conductor of the Toronto Symphony, Gerron captured their haunting eyes and their despair. One of Theresienstadt's most illustrious prisoners, Alice's friend Rabbi Leo Baeck, was shown in a staged lecture. The background music was the aching melancholy of the slow movement of Mendelssohn's Trio for Piano, Violin, and Cello in D Minor, otherwise banned by the Nazis throughout occupied Europe. The footage also included a few frames of a pretty girl who turned toward the camera with a stilted smile as she watered a garden. There were vacant stares on the faces of the elderly as they sat on "park benches" purportedly enjoying the view and terrified looks of the youngest children, who were anxiously riding hobby horses as if they were trying to gallop into the arms of their mothers, who had already disappeared. In a shot of the audience for *Brundibár*, Gerron focused on a skinny boy who was not wearing a shirt. And even in the normally joyful final scene of the opera, the unsmiling children looked frightened and hopeless as they mechanically sang the chorus. The truth of Gerron's film shone through for anyone who had the courage to see.

As soon as Gerron wrapped the film, on orders from Reich Minister of Propaganda Dr. Joseph Goebbels, a sealed train left Theresienstadt bearing its final cargo of more than two thousand prisoners who had participated in the production. When the train came to a stop in Auschwitz, the doors were unlatched and the name Gerron was blasted from the bullhorns.

"Kurt Gerron, *heraus*" (get out). The other prisoners watched as Gerron made his way out of the cattle car and into the hands of SS guards. According to eyewitnesses, he looked neither right nor left. Gerron had been singled out for "special treatment," on orders from Gestapo headquarters, to make certain the director would not talk. With his head held high and without looking back, Gerron was marched directly into the gas chamber. He was forty-seven. Miraculously the bass soloist Karel Berman was one of the very few on that transport to survive Auschwitz.

Gerron's film was edited in Prague, and a copy was sent to Berlin, where it was destroyed before Germany surrendered. It was only in late 1945 that the chief cameraman, Ivan Frič, who had been partially protected from the murderous truths of Theresienstadt, learned what had happened to Gerron and the masses of Czechs in the film.

After the war, fragments of the film Frič shot for Gerron—including scenes from *Brundibár* and Haas's piece for string orchestra—were found in a Czech production house. Researchers continue to discover additional pieces of the film in archives, so someday most of Gerron's film may be pieced together from the extant storyboards.

Today Alice asks, "How can anyone look at the faces in the film without seeing the truth?" Answering her own question, she adds, "We all see only what we want to see." In the words that one courageous prisoner managed to whisper to one of the Red Cross visitors: "Open your eyes. See what they do not show. Look."

TEN

Snapshots

Alice lives amid her few remaining photographs and mementos. Her one-room flat, humble in its timeworn simplicity, is a kind of cocoon carrying her memories forward day by day. Her furniture is a collection of unmatched items, from the upholstered green velour chair to the metal tables that look as if they are discards from someone else on moving day. Her antique Steinway upright piano is centered against the long wall. Without design, each visible remembrance intertwines with another, invoking a portrait of Alice's life.

When one first enters Alice's studio apartment, a large framed portrait of a dashing, youngish man wearing an eye patch catches the eye. It is a photograph of Alice's most beloved piano teacher, Václav Štěpán. He had lost his left eye in an accident in the military during World War I, but in no way did this injury hinder his artistry; in fact, Štěpán could deliver lengthy explanations of the value of limited vision for musicians. He was regarded as one of Czechoslovakia's finest and most daring pianists and was highly sought after as a teacher for both piano and composition.

Štěpán was one of the first people Alice tried to find when she returned to Prague in 1945, and she was heartbroken to learn that he had died of cancer shortly before the city's liberation. Professor Štěpán was so influential—musically and personally—to her that she even named her baby after him. Štěpán's widow had given the framed photograph to Alice as a memento.

In addition to Štěpán's portrait, there are pictures of Rafi everywhere in Alice's room. The center photograph on her piano shows Rafi with Pablo Casals and was taken in the summer of 1965 at the acclaimed Marlboro Music Festival. Rafi had played in a performance of Bach's Suite no. 2 in B Minor conducted by Casals. Two weeks later Rafi was the cellist for the Boccherini Quintet, and this time Casals was a member of his audience. Alice was more thrilled than Rafi when he wrote to her about the concerts; she understood how lasting the time in the presence of the great Casals could be. When she wrote back to her son in the States, she reminded him to keep careful notes each day. He must remember every word the maestro uttered.

The weeks Rafi spent at Marlboro, working with the

greatest musicians from across the globe in the forested Green Mountains of Vermont, were unforgettable. Founded by Rudolf Serkin to promote chamber music concerts in his new country, the festival was uniquely democratic in that the young artists played in ensembles with the great and the famous. Serkin, who was born in Czechoslovakia in 1903, the same year as Alice, was already a world-famous pianist; he and several members of his family had been fortunate to escape to the United States in 1939. Rafi never told Serkin that he was a Holocaust survivor. For Rafi, the experience was all about music. The violinist Jaime Laredo vividly remembers Rafi not only as a fine cellist but as an ebullient young man full of humor.

A Hanukkah menorah stands prominently among the photographs on Alice's piano like an honor guard, the only symbol of Jewish life that she brought from Israel when she immigrated. Geneviève, Rafi's widow, describes Alice joyfully lighting the candles for the eight nights of Hanukkah—the word itself means dedication—for her son and her grandchildren, just as her family did when she was a child in Prague. On the wall next to the piano is a drawing of a string quartet that includes two members of Alice's family, reworked from a prewar photograph: her brother Paul is playing first violin, and her husband, Leopold, is on second violin. According to Alice it was a first-rate amateur quartet whose Thursday night rehearsals were never to be missed.

A stack of old musical scores sits on the faded green velvet seat of the piano bench. More music is piled on the floor, and standing open above the piano keys is a large hardbound score, its fragile yellowed pages showing rips and tears from endless use. It is the piano part of Beethoven's Spring sonata for violin and piano. Alice played this sonata many times with violinists in European concerts before the war; in Theresienstadt she performed it with violinists who had been members of the Czech Philharmonic Orchestra; and in Israel she played it often as well. In London, Alice still returns repeatedly to this work. "Beethoven is a miracle," she says. "Beethoven is not only melody, he is full, deep—intense." She explains that in the piece the violin and the piano are engaged in a democratic dialogue. The theme is tossed back and forth, intertwining the instruments in respectful and intimate conversation. Each instrument plays an equal role. Neither stands alone, nor can one exist without the other. Alice points out that Beethoven did not title the work "Spring"—the nickname became popular soon after the sonata was published, probably because of its sunny, tender melodies.

Above Alice's single bed are two small but colorful oil paintings of the hills of Jerusalem, a reminder of the land that gave her refuge and a fresh start, and where she spent her happiest years. Nothing in the room serves as a reminder of her Czech roots; she feels few personal ties with the city of her childhood. Her home, her school, and her family have all disappeared.

On the wall directly across from her bed is an unframed oil painting of her son with his cello. Edna, one of Alice's multigifted piano students in Jerusalem, painted the lifelike oil from a photograph. Rafi's pensive face is the first image Alice sees in the morning and the last before she closes her eyes at night. She says that the painting brings her so close to her son that she can nearly hear the sound of his cello. Edna flew to London from Israel to give the portrait to Alice for her hundredth birthday.

A closer look around the room shows that mementos of Rafi dominate the space. Stored under the television are videotapes of Rafi playing his cello or conducting. And even the small white electric fan that rests on top of books is a reminder of him. Rafi gave it to her to help her get through hot days more comfortably. Alice says that nearly every week she would receive a present from her son. Tossed over the back of her chair are woolen throws and a shawl Rafi gave her for the extra cold days.

A few books on music, along with books by Franz Kafka and the Austrian writer Stefan Zweig's *World of Yesterday,* are within easy reach on the small table beside Alice's bed. Zweig's book, which she has read and reread countless times, was a gift from her beloved Michal Mareš, who gave it to her in 1945. Through the many intervening years, in Israel and in London, *The World of Yesterday* has been her constant companion. Originally published in German in Sweden in 1943—it had been banned in all Nazi-occupied countries because the author was Jewish—initially the book was for Alice a connection to her past, a beautiful portrayal of the world of her childhood, in which music, literature, and the life of the mind were revered. As a young woman Alice had even met Zweig, who was connected to her circle through his friendship with Gustav Mahler and Richard Strauss.

Zweig's early portrayal of Hitler's rise to power haunted Alice. She would ask herself over and over: how could Zweig's vision have been so acute when most of the world took so little heed? "Nothing misled the German intellectuals as much as his lack of education into believing that Hitler was still only the beer-hall agitator who never could become a real danger," Zweig wrote. "Then came the Reichstag fire, parliament disappeared, Goering let loose his hordes, and at one blow all of justice in Germany was smashed. . . . National Socialism in its unscrupulous technique of deceit was wary about disclosing the full extent of its aims before the world had become inured. Thus they practiced their method carefully: only a small dose to begin with then a brief pause . . . to see whether the world conscience would still digest this dose. . . . The doses became progressively stronger until all of Europe finally perished from them." Still, "everybody had a ready-made phrase: That cannot last long. . . . It was the self deception that we practice because of reluctance to abandon our accustomed life." Discussing Zweig's account of those days, Alice says, "*Ja,* the world did not want to look at the truth until it was too late. And we should have known."

When Alice later learned what had happened to Austria's most famous writer, *The World of Yesterday* took on an even greater meaning for her. Zweig, a pacifist, had been reluctant to leave his home in Vienna, although the nation had become his avowed enemy. After fleeing for his life, he was given permanent residency in England, and he then spent time in the United States before deciding to settle in Petrópolis, Brazil, where he lived during his last five months. When the Nazis invaded the Soviet Union, in 1941, Zweig believed that a dark curtain had descended and that Hitler and the reign of evil would conquer the world he knew. Without hope, unable to adapt to a new country, Zweig made a conscious decision to end his life. Alice wishes that he had been more patient, had not descended into total despair. "He was so wise, he could have given so much more," she says. These thoughts helped to strengthen her resolve as she continued to face her own challenges. Alice muses that if Zweig had been older maybe he would have found more hope. Nodding her head, she murmurs, "Only when we are so very old do we realize the beauty of life."

On a shelf Alice keeps two shoe boxes filled with her mementos. The first holds her remaining family photographs: her wedding picture taken outside Prague's City Hall, a photo of her brother Paul, several snapshots of herself before the war, and a tiny black-and-white image of her mother as a young woman. A small plaque in the box was given to Alice by the government of Israel—she recalls neither the occasion nor the purpose of the award. A bearded man in a small photograph, probably taken by her mother, turns out to be Sigmund Freud. Freud had been born in Moravia and had met Sofie through mutual family friends in Vienna. In the late 1920s, when Alice and her mother visited a relative in Vienna, where he was living at the time near Freud's office on the Berggasse, they would often run into Freud on their walks, and the famous doctor would always stop to exchange a few words with them. The second box holds two four-by-six-inch scrapbooks, which have survived the war and Alice's relocation to two new countries. Most of the pages are covered with small clippings from the Czech German newspaper, which Alice had carefully pasted onto the pages, reviews of her concerts.

Alice admits that through the years she has given away many of her keepsakes, and that nearly everything she collected before the war has been lost. Still, she is grateful for the few photographs she has around her. And her lifeline, her Steinway piano. "They make me happy. Every day. What is lost? Sometimes people bring me a little picture or a letter, an envelope. . . ." She pauses. "It does not matter. My memories are always with me. My life is in my mind."

Remembering her study of ancient Greek philosophers, Alice quotes, "Memory is the scribe of the soul." As she taps her forehead with the third finger of her right hand, she whispers, "Here."

INTERLUDE

Old Age

"It's not so bad!" Alice says in her most dramatic way about her advanced age. "When people come to visit, people much younger than myself, many like to tell me how bad things are, their money problems, their aches and pains. And worst of all they tell me how terrible old age is. 'It's so terrible, so terrible.' And I shock them by disagreeing. 'It's not so terrible. And I'm older than you. Rather than dwell on problems, why not look for life's gifts?' Every day is a present. Beautiful."

She says that, just because she is old in years, she is not irrelevant. And more insistently Alice says, "My mind is young. My emotions and my imagination are still young." Then with a whimsical bit of laughter, "Of course, I do have some experience."

Alice becomes even more animated in the presence of

attractive young men; she enjoys admitting, "You cannot see the real me inside my wrinkled skin, the life of my emotions. What you see is only the outer face of a very old woman."

When a Czech Television crew arrived at her London home for an interview in the summer of 2006, Alice was neatly dressed in a pale blue knit skirt and matching short-sleeved sweater. As always she was wearing canvas sneakers. That day she had chosen white ones. The chief cameraman and the director, both in their late twenties, were over six feet tall and handsome. She greeted them in Czech, giggling girlishly, and insisted that they help themselves to the tea and cookies that she had already laid out; she then excused herself quickly. About ten minutes later a vivacious Alice reappeared wearing red sneakers, red lipstick, and a necklace. Later, when asked what was the single most important thing in the world, a most serious Alice answered, "Love, love, of course." Then, pausing to laugh heartily, she wagged her finger at the director and added, "But I don't mean sex."

Alice is always ready for something new: a new thought, a new book, a new idea, new people. Her curiosity is insatiable. Well beyond an age when many begin to turn away from everything different or unfamiliar, she welcomes nearly everything innovative. Alice recently asked to try Jacqueline Danson's iPhone. Jackie, the granddaughter of a Czech friend, watched fascinated as Alice's 107-year-old finger manipulated the keypad. And when Alice lies in bed, she exercises her mind by mentally playing entire pieces. While she is sitting and talking, her fingers move continually. When asked what she is playing, she quips, "Bach, of course."

Even though Alice has no desire for anything materialistic and has probably not bought new clothes in decades, she is both interested in and aware of fashion. She notices what others wear, touches the fabric, and offers compliments. And her attitude on sex is nothing short of astonishing considering her age and background. Her former student Ester Maron recently introduced Alice to her daughter Michal, who is in her late twenties. Learning that the girl was a cellist in the Haifa Symphony, Alice asked her if there was a man in her life. Michal replied that she had just broken up with her most recent boyfriend. "Good," Alice said. "Keep it that way. Have sex, have fun, have someone in your life, but don't tie yourself down in marriage. Cherish your freedom and your music." In fact, whenever Alice learns that a young woman or an older single woman has a lover, she gives unsolicited advice: "Oh, that is good, but make certain that he lives in his own place. You should see him only when and if it is good for you. Keep your freedom, take care of your career, your life." Spinoza seems to be present, like a shadow, whispering in Alice's ear as her guide. Her favorite philosopher wrote that sexual passion usually leads to unhappiness. He felt that if a love is to last it must be based on reason and friendship rather than uncontrolled passions.

Today Alice follows Spinoza's profound directive: "Do not weep; do not wax indignant. Understand." She believes that understanding is the pillar of all learning and the essential foundation for peace—in our hearts, our cities, and our world. Before people rush to confront a neighbor, before soldiers rush to fight, "can't we try first to understand each other?" she asks. "Since when has making enemies been a solution?" Having lived through so many wars, Alice is hardly naïve when she talks about understanding. She is aware that you do not need to like or agree with someone in order to understand his point of view. Alice emphasizes, "Don't stand there and cry. Understand."

For Alice the philosopher, Spinoza vindicated her thoughts in his many volumes on reason. As she faces what are inevitably the last years of her life, she does not fritter away her cherished time with fears of death and worries about the unknown. Death, for Alice, is not unfamiliar. Again she accepts Spinoza's reasoning that death and life are part of the same infinity or God. According to Alice, "We come from and return to Infinity." She adds that she believes that "the soul lives on without the body." As she listens repeatedly to Mahler's Second Symphony, Alice finds consolation in the song for alto soloist, *"Urlicht"* (primal light), at the beginning of the fourth movement. Perhaps for Alice *"Urlicht"*—with its opening words "I come from God and I will return to God"—has always been her spiritual theme song. Loosely quoting Spinoza, she says, "Things are as they are supposed to be. I am still here—never too old so long as I breathe to wonder, to learn, and, yes, still to teach. Curiosity—interest in others, and, above all, music. This is life."

ELEVEN

Man in the Glass Booth

On an April morning in Jerusalem in 1961, walking arm in arm with her friend Edith Steiner-Kraus—the pianist who had accompanied many of the performances of Verdi's Requiem in Theresienstadt—Alice entered the heavily guarded chambers of the opening of the trial of Nazi SS Lieutenant Colonel Adolf Eichmann, and the two women took their designated seats. Alice had never before been in a courtroom.

The head prosecutor for the trial, Gideon Hausner, attorney general for the State of Israel, had invited her to attend the proceedings. She and Hausner had met through his daughter, who was one of Alice's youngest piano students. After her lessons Hausner, himself a remarkable pianist, would frequently sit with Alice and play duets for fun. Although he was not a criminal lawyer, Hausner had drafted

the indictment against Eichmann, charging him with mul-
tiple counts of war crimes and crimes against humanity.
Golda Meir, then foreign minister, explained that the trial
"was not, in any sense, a question of revenge . . . but those
who remained alive—and generations still unborn—deserve,
if nothing else, that the world know, in all its dreadful detail,
what was done to the Jews of Europe and by whom." The
Nobel Peace Prize laureate Elie Wiesel, as a young journalist,
covered the trial for the Jewish newspaper *The Forward.*
Later he wrote in his *Memoirs,* "If only the defendant could
be declared irrevocably inhuman, expelled from the human
species. It irritated me to think of Eichmann as human."

In Beit Ha'am, a large auditorium temporarily outfitted
as the courtroom for this singular trial, before three presid-
ing judges, Eichmann sat in a bulletproof glass booth specially constructed by the Israelis for his protection against
the anger of the crowd. It was the first trial to be broadcast
worldwide on television.

SS Obersturmbannführer Adolf Eichmann was three
years younger than Alice. His ordinary middle-class German family had attended services at the Lutheran church
every Sunday. Although he was never more than a mediocre
student and eventually dropped out of high school, Eichmann was noted for his exceptional obedience to authority.
Mesmerized by the nationalistic fervor of its members, he
had joined the Nazi Party in 1932, and when he lost his me-

nial job working for a subsidiary of Standard Oil, he found employment and a new career in the feared and powerful SS. He was a man they could trust. Eichmann married a German woman and lived for several years in Prague as he quickly advanced from sergeant to lieutenant colonel, to the top of the Central Office for Jewish Emigration. By 1939 he was back in Berlin, where he was appointed the head of Gestapo Section IV B4, or Jewish Affairs. The SS had discovered his talent for organization and, more important, his ambition to succeed no matter the task. In 1942 Eichmann was given the new position of transportation administrator of the Final Solution to the Jewish Question; he controlled all the trains and managed the logistics of the mass deportations of Jews across Europe to Hitler's death camps. He planned the seizure and disposition of Jewish property to make certain that his office benefited from the profits. Eichmann alone decided how many, in what order, in which countries, and when the Jews would be murdered.

And Eichmann was personally responsible for the establishment of Theresienstadt as a way station to hold Jews he would efficiently deliver to Auschwitz and other death camps. He made more than one inspection tour of his model camp. Alice's brother Paul, who was in a small orchestra that was ordered to perform for the Nazi high command, saw Eichmann during his final visit, in late 1944.

Israeli intelligence finally caught up with Eichmann fifteen years after the war. He had escaped Germany with the help of officials of the Catholic Church and had been living in Buenos Aires under an assumed name, Ricardo Klement, with his wife, Vera, and four sons. A Mossad agent named Peter Malkin had been observing his movements for several days before his capture. Watching him come home from work and get down on the floor to play with his youngest child, Malkin found the scene particularly disturbing—it was so ordinary. After Eichmann was caught getting off a bus on his way home from work, Malkin spent hours talking with him. Malkin had lost his parents and many other relatives in the Holocaust, and he wanted to know how any human being could have conceived of and committed such atrocities. Eichmann showed no emotion and insisted that he had never killed anyone. It was a known fact that near the end of the war Himmler had ordered the killing to stop and the evidence to be destroyed. Enraged, Eichmann had defied the Reichsführer's orders and had sped up the deportations of thousands of Hungarian Jews marked for death.

Eichmann repeatedly claimed, "I was just responsible for transportation." Malkin told him that his own cousin, his best childhood friend, was six years old and had blond hair and blue eyes just like Eichmann's son when Eichmann "killed him in Auschwitz." According to Malkin, Eichmann commented, "Yes, but he was Jewish, wasn't he?"

Without apology or regret, Eichmann would stick to his defense that he was only a "transmitter." Elie Wiesel later wrote, "I could not take my eyes off the defendant, who sat in his glass cage impassively taking notes. He seemed utterly unmoved by the recitation of the crimes against humanity and the Jewish people of which he was accused. He looked like an ordinary man. I was told he ate heartily and slept normally. Considering the crushing pressures of the trial, he seemed to bear up well. Neither the prosecutors nor the judges were able to break him." Wiesel went on, "The accused Eichmann spoke freely, unafraid. He cited documents and figures, he held back nothing—he was desperately bent on saving his neck."

Portraying himself as only a bureaucrat who was powerless, Eichmann testified: "I never did anything, great or small, without obtaining in advance express instructions from Adolf Hitler or any of my superiors." At one point he even said, "I regret nothing." During his trial, he acknowledged the trait of obedience that his parents had instilled in him: "Now that I look back, I realize that a life predicated on being obedient and taking orders is a very comfortable life indeed. Living in such a way reduces to a minimum one's need to think."

When Hausner cross-examined the defendant, he asked if Eichmann considered himself guilty of the murder of millions of Jews. Eichmann replied: "Legally not, but in the human sense . . . yes, for I am guilty of having deported them."

Alice listened to survivors describe inconceivable horrors far worse than what she had experienced in the Theresienstadt ghetto. Dressed in civilian clothes, a suit and tie—he was forbidden to wear his Nazi uniform and decorations—Eichmann looked coldly arrogant. Alice searched his face and posture for some sign of remorse. Even as Hausner produced as evidence a quote by Eichmann stating, "I will leap into my grave laughing because the feeling that I have five million human beings on my conscience is for me a source of extraordinary satisfaction," the defendant seemed proud of his role and his exemplary discharge of duties for the Third Reich.

The political philosopher Hannah Arendt, herself a refugee from Nazi Germany, who covered the trial for *The New Yorker* magazine, said that she found Eichmann perfectly normal, only blindly ambitious. The SS offered him the unimaginable respect and power that he could not attain in a civil society. Explaining the "banality of evil," Arendt wrote, "The sad truth is that most evil is done by people who never make up their minds to be good or evil. . . . The trouble with Eichmann was precisely that so many were like him, and that the many were neither perverted nor sadistic, that they were, and still are, terribly and terrifyingly normal."

Although the trial lasted sixteen weeks, Alice attended for a mere handful of days. She found to her horror that she was feeling pity, not only for the wasted, destructive life of the heartless man in the glass box but also for the entire German nation. The Germans had awarded Sigmund Freud their distinguished Goethe Prize for literature in 1930, and only three years later, because he was Jewish, the Nazis had marked his writings for burning. Freud had escaped at the last moment to England, his name joining a small list of other great Jewish intellects who had managed to flee: Martin Buber to Palestine, Albert Einstein and others to America.

Alice thought of Goethe's words memorized in her childhood: "Hatred is something peculiar. You will always find it strongest and most violent where there is the lowest degree of culture." What had gone so wrong in the educated culture and nations of Beethoven, Schiller, Goethe, and Zweig, the world and ideals of her youth? Alice would come to agree with Hannah Arendt that "there is a strange interdependence between thoughtlessness and evil." Later the Jewish philosopher Martin Buber would equate the rise of Nazism with an eclipse of God.

But the intense anger of the crowd both in and outside the courtroom as they waited impatiently for justice to be served also disturbed Alice. What was justice? Buber and many others had argued against the death penalty for Eichmann. No court in the world could bring back the lives that had been lost. Sadness overwhelmed Alice. Schiller's words flooded her: "Wouldst thou know thyself, observe the actions of others. Wouldst thou other men know, look thou within thine own heart. "

Unable to voice her feelings, Alice left the court.

She spent the rest of the day and evening in her private form of prayer, playing her piano. She played Bach—whom she named the philosopher of music—finding perfection in his most minute twists and turns. "No matter how many years you have known one work of Bach or how many hours you have practiced, you can always strive to reach a higher level. Bach is a whole universe. Infinite," she explains. She found similarities between life in all of its unforeseen highs and lows and his music: his uncanny dissonances, which might be inserted in passing on the way to a resolution and are sometimes nearly unnoticeable, and which in other phrases are proclaimed in a momentary burst of joy. Beyond spoken language, beyond national borders, beyond worldly concerns, beyond hate, music was her language, the language of humanity. Bach brought Alice to a state of peace. Later she would frequently say, "Music brings us to paradise."

Alice is convinced that we are not genetically programmed to hate one another. But she now recognizes that anyone, anywhere, and at any time can adopt hatred and, worse, can infect others with its venom. Hatred that may begin with one person, like a single pebble cast into a lake, can spread to larger and larger groups, and even to entire nations. While the Holocaust ended with the defeat of the Nazis in 1945, Alice observes that the world has changed very little since then. The metamorphosis of individual prejudice into group hatred and killing is still happening in the twenty-first century. Remembering her own first encounter with hatred as a child, when a stranger called her a "dirty Jew," Alice emphasizes, "Each individual can choose good or evil. It is up to us, each one of us." She thinks of the famous Protestant composer Max Bruch, who, when criticized for using racial slurs, answered, "I only said what everyone else was saying."

Alice never tires of pointing out, "We are responsible for our actions and our words. And each of us must vigilantly guard against prejudice and hatred in our own minds and with the words that fall from our lips. No one is exempt. No one. Hitler could not have come to power except in the climate of excessive hatred."

While her words may appear simplistic, the deeper truth she divines is undisputable. "Hatred only begets hatred."

TWELVE

No Harsh Words

"How can any woman ever be unhappy after she has seen her infant's first smile? This is a miracle. My son's birth was the happiest day of my life. My most awe-inspiring moment was when I saw my baby smile for the first time." The philosopher in Alice adds, "He was happy because he did not know unhappiness. He did not want for things he did not need. I can say that it was my greatest privilege to raise my son." Although Hitler had become Chancellor of Germany four years before Rafi was born in 1937, Alice was determined that as long as she lived she would be strong for her son. "A mother's love is the child's only fortress against the world, come what may," she says.

As a baby, Rafi would sleep peacefully while Alice practiced. By the time he was three years old he would make his own fingers fly about in imitation of his mother's hands.

One day he was busy playing his imaginary piano while Alice was rehearsing songs by Schumann with a singer when he suddenly began to cry. "What is wrong? What happened?" Alice asked as she lifted him onto her lap. Sobbing he said, "The music is so beautiful." For the rest of the rehearsal Rafi sat quietly between his mother's arms as she played. That evening Alice told her husband what had happened. "Our son is talented," she announced to Leopold.

At that time, the majority of traditional European parents believed in strict, even harsh discipline of their children. Alice was different. She accepted her sensitive child as a full human being. From the beginning Alice was aware that the tone of her voice and every word she uttered could influence her growing son.

Alice became a single mother after Rafi's seventh birthday, when her husband was sent on to Auschwitz and she and Rafi remained in Theresienstadt. Until the war ended she raised her son in the concentration camp, surrounded by filth, disease, and death. "The hardest thing for me in the camp was to listen to my child cry from hunger and have nothing, nothing to give to him," she recalls. "This was terrible. And his questions. How should I answer? Rafi continually asked, 'What is war?' 'Why can't we go home?' 'What is a Jew?' 'Why are we Jews?' "

Since Rafi was only six when they arrived in Theresienstadt, Alice was permitted to keep him with her in the women's quarters. They slept together in her narrow wooden bunk. As the days turned into weeks and months, Alice understood this significant blessing. "When a child is held close to you and can sense the warmth of your body, the child feels secure." This, she explains, is true regardless of the circumstances, but in Theresienstadt it was critical for her child's well-being. After the war, when Alice read the philosophy of Martin Buber, his words affirmed her belief: "The world is not comprehensible, but it is embraceable: through the embracing of one of its beings." After Leopold was deported to Auschwitz, Rafi would often voice his constant fear, "Now that Papa is gone, if they take you away I will be all alone in this world." "Alone in this world," Alice repeats. "How did this little boy have the idea of a larger world?" She assured Rafi that she would never leave him, and in comforting her son, she intensified her own determination to survive. Protecting Rafi became her mission. "I made up stories constantly. I was laughing. Never did I let my son see my fear or worry. And tears had no place in a concentration camp. Laughter was our only medicine."

When Alice and Rafi had first entered Theresienstadt's gates, in 1943, soldiers with drawn machine guns guarded the entrance. Fortunately the Nazi guard did not understand Czech when Rafi announced in his loudest voice, "Mommy,

I don't like it here. I want to go home." From that moment Alice invented fairy tales and stories to quell his anxiety and pass the time. She asked him to imagine that they were on-stage in a play. The bad witch had forced them to take the wrong train, and they were waiting for the good soldiers to rescue them. When Rafi saw his mother smiling and even laughing through it all, he could only think things must not be so bad. When they ate the watery soup that was served for both lunch and dinner, Alice told a story of a king's ban-quet where they were given all they could eat. Rafi joined in and pretended he was eating mounds of potatoes and doz-ens of his favorite chocolates.

But Rafi was also full of daring childish energy. To save his life, Alice managed to discipline him with reason, not punishment. "Giving your child instructions in a serious tone is very different from using angry sounding words," she explains. For Alice harsh words send a message that is dis-missive and unloving. To survive, "a child must never, never doubt your love."

When Rafi was offered the role of the sparrow in *Brundibár*, the conductor, Rudi Freudenfeld, was surprised at how quickly and perfectly on pitch he learned his solo. Working in the factory, Alice could not supervise him dur-ing the rehearsals, so the job of watching over the rambunc-tious boy fell to fourteen-year-old Ela Weissberger—who sang the role of the cat—and to several of her friends. Yet Rafi never missed his moment to sing, and he never missed a note.

After the war Alice refused to talk to anyone about their days in the concentration camp because she feared that Rafi might overhear their conversation, and she wanted him to forget those horrific years. Years later, when Rafi reconnected with Ela as an adult, he asked her, "Tell me how I was in *Brundibár*. I remember nothing."

Rafi learned by example; he never used harsh words with his mother. He quickly adapted to his new home and new culture in Israel. He excelled in school and absorbed Hebrew like a sponge, and he was always interested in the world around him. Alice never needed to remind him to do his homework or to practice. Because of his mother's work schedule, he spent many hours alone. He learned not only to accept solitude but to relish it. When he decided that he wanted to have a Bar Mitzvah, he worked hard with his tutor, and he was rewarded with a shiny new bicycle.

Until he left home for his military service, Rafi would begin every day, before school, with an hour's piano lesson with his mother. He also studied cello at the Jerusalem Academy of Music. According to Alice, "He was an excellent pianist, excellent." She loves to relate how he wowed his fellow students when, barely age ten, he played not one but two Beethoven sonatas in a school program. Yet he was drawn more to the rich voice of the cello. His progress on that instrument was so rapid that, by the time he was in high school, he was capable of performing much of the difficult repertoire.

The year 1954 was Rafi's lucky year. The renowned French cellist Paul Tortelier, a Catholic, was compelled to move, at least temporarily, to a kibbutz with his wife, two children, two students, his mother, and his sister. When Tortelier had played a concert in Israel, Vera Stern, the wife of the violinist Isaac Stern, suggested that they visit her favorite kibbutz, Ma'abarot, near Netanya, between Tel Aviv and Haifa. Tortelier and his wife, Maud, fell in love with the kibbutz's beauty and tranquillity, while the ideals of the new Israeli nation exerted a powerful pull on them. Not only did he want to help in some way to build the country but he turned down an entire year of concerts in order to work unpaid picking grapefruits and bananas in the orchards of Kibbutz Ma'abarot and serving dinner once a week. And of course he continued to teach. Tortelier would later describe the experience in his autobiography: "We began a simple life: just love and work . . . the man who collected rubbish was on an equal status with a professor of science. Everyone wore the same clothes, ate the same food and was treated equally. For a man like me . . . such a life is ideal. . . . You have whatever you need because . . . you don't need so much in life. We acquire a lot of unnecessary things whether through fear, temptation or habit. . . . It was wonderful to experience . . . the radiant contact between people who share daily the same love of nature, work and beauty in complete equality and simplicity."

Rafi's cello teacher arranged his audition. Encouraged by his mother, Rafi traveled two hours by bus on dusty roads to play for the great cellist, who was instantly fascinated by the young man's talent and musicianship. After giving him a trial lesson, Tortelier advised Rafi to complete his high school studies in Jerusalem and then come to France to study with him at the Paris Conservatory. Tortelier added the promise of a scholarship.

Rafi received the grant from the conservatory in 1958. But he and Alice faced an interesting challenge. How would they communicate? The telephone was too expensive. Although Alice spoke Hebrew, she was able to read and write it at only an elementary level. Rafi could write neither Czech nor German. They decided that it would be best to write to each other in Hebrew. Alice once again began studying Hebrew and became more fluent with each of the many letters that she wrote to her son.

Rafi graduated from the conservatory four years later with a coveted first prize.

Over the next few years Rafi would win many competitions, including the Piatigorsky Artist Award in Boston, second prize at the 1963 Munich International Cello Competition, and first prize at the 1965 competition in Santiago de Compostela. With all of the concerts that ensued, his international career was launched.

Security came to Rafi with an offer to serve as head of the cello department at the Royal Northern College of Music in Manchester, England, where he remained for twenty-two years. He also conducted the First Chamber Orchestra at the Royal College of Music in London, where he made his home for the rest of his life, and he and his wife, Geneviève, founded an annual summer chamber music festival at Gex, in the French countryside, where they had a second home. Alice would frequently travel with Rafi as his accompanist in the late sixties and early seventies. Together they played cello-piano concerts throughout Europe and even ventured as far as the United States and South America, while he continued to be awarded prizes and honors, including the Grosser Sudetendeutscher Kulturpreis 2000 in Nuremberg, and Britain's highest recognition of a musician by the queen mother, who made him an Honorable Member of the Royal College of Music. But the most meaningful reward may have been one that was not given to him; rather, his legacy as a teacher was honored when one of his students won second prize in the International Rostropovitch Cello Competition.

But no matter the heights he achieved as cellist and teacher, Rafi would remain forever grateful to his own teacher, mentor, and friend Paul Tortelier. In 2000 Rafi organized a Tenth Anniversary Memorial Concert in London's Wigmore Hall in honor of the great cellist, who had died in 1990 in the village of Villarceaux, near Paris. The memorial was to be Rafi's last big project, as he too died only one year later. Tortelier's idealism in music and life not only influenced Rafi's artistry but also reinforced the foundation built on his mother's musical as well as moral principles. Tortelier, who happened to have been born on Bach's birthday, March 21, had shared Alice's belief in the power of that composer. He wrote, "The art of Johann Sebastian Bach represents the highest achievement of mankind: it is sovereign . . . as is the idea of universal peace. We must work together against the peril of nuclear war if we want our grandchildren to be able to listen to Bach's music."

When Alice learned that Rafi was engaged to be married to a young French pianist, Sylvie Ott, whom he had met at the Paris Conservatory, she was thrilled to welcome her new daughter-in-law into the family. When they produced two beautiful grandsons, David and Ariel, Alice was ecstatic. Some years after, though, Alice noticed that her son seemed generally unhappy. He and Sylvie argued bitterly about insignificant details. Although they didn't complain or speak of their problems, Alice could not help but feel the underlying hostility and ever-increasing distance between the two. One day as they were sitting around her kitchen table in

London, Alice looked them both straight in the face and said, "You are both wonderful people, but together you are unhappy. It makes no sense for you to continue this way, and besides, the atmosphere is detrimental for the children." Rafi and Sylvie looked at each other in amazement. They could hardly believe that Alice, the grandmother of their children, would suggest separation.

Rafi asked, "Are you saying that you think we should divorce?"

"It seems you have little choice," Alice replied.

"But we can't afford a lawyer," Rafi protested.

"Why do you need an attorney? You are both reasonable people. Let's work this out right now. I will act as your lawyer." Alice reached for pen and paper and, following their suggestions, began to draft an agreement that both could live with.

The informal family meeting resulted in a quick, fair, and amicable divorce. To further prove her unbiased support for both her son and his wife, Alice paid the fees for processing the papers for court approval. Not only did the young couple avoid both the acrimony and the costs of opposing attorneys but Alice's diplomacy extended into the future. Today, ten years after Raphaël's death and twenty years after the divorce, Sylvie continues to check on Alice by phone.

When speaking of her son's divorce, Alice says, "Why should it be so hateful, so complicated? By getting married my son and his wife had made a youthful mistake. No rabbi, priest, or judge can guarantee that a marriage can or should last forever. Their life together was becoming more and more miserable, as each wanted or needed something different from the marriage. Divorce was simply the logical solution. And it was better for their two little boys than growing up facing the example of discontented parents at home. Common sense, it was simply common sense."

Closing her eyes for a moment to think, Alice continues, "Now that I have lived so long to see my grandsons grown, and now that both of Rafi's wives are older women, I know that it was the right decision. Yes, I am proud of that. Most people say that you must never interfere in your children's lives. But sometimes they need your help, a little push . . . *Ja*, your child is always your child."

Toward the end of his life Rafi wrote a small testimony describing his commitment to his art. Alice memorized his words, which she often quotes aloud: "I am not ambitious to be the best, not at all. I want to show people the great beauty of music. One of the greatest pleasures of music is to make other people listen to it; to feel, for just a moment, a tiny part of an ideal world in which everything is good, beautiful . . . Music is a bliss. Music brings us an island of peace." Describing him as an adult, Alice says of her son, "He almost never used the pronoun 'I.' When he was grown he did not talk much, but when he did you listened. My son was not ambitious or jealous in the usual way. My son was generous with his praise of others."

Alice describes the night Rafi died, after playing a concert in Israel. "He played a wonderful concert, all Beethoven, that evening with his Salomon Trio. He was happy. After the concert he told his friends that he did not feel well, and they took him to a hospital." Alice explains that he was diagnosed with an iliac aneurysm. He was given anesthesia, because the doctors had to operate to try to save his life. "He never woke up," Alice recounts. "I am thankful that he did not suffer. He had a beautiful last day. I am thankful that his last memories were of the music. I am thankful that he did not know that he was going to die so that he did not have to be afraid."

Acknowledging her son's death on November 13, 2001, just thirteen days before her ninety-eighth birthday, was the trial of her life. Her friends and family worried. How could she survive this cruelest of blows? But Alice set a formidable example of accepting what she could not change with love and dignity. She was concerned for the others—for Geneviève and her grandsons.

Rafi's funeral service was mostly music, just as his life had been. A few people spoke briefly, and then several of his friends and colleagues sat around his open grave with their cellos and played. Nearly every month Alice visits Rafi's grave on the arm of her grandson Ariel. The simple headstone is engraved in Hebrew. Asked if she believes in prayer, Alice answers, "Yes, it helps us in a crisis when we need it most." Still, she never indulges in self-pity. "After all, I am not the only mother who has lost her son. Maybe I draw from the strength of the great pianist Clara Schumann, who one hundred years before me lost two of her children, Felix and Julia. Music kept her going until she closed her eyes for the last time."

Alice looks back at Rafi's premature death and admits she is glad that he missed the sorrows and pain of old age. Looking around the room at his many photographs, she says that the pictures remind her that he is dead. "Look at that painting with his cello. It is beautiful, but it is a painting of a man who is no more." Inserting a video into her VCR player, Alice smiles and says, "Now he lives." She watches a performance of Rafi conducting *Brundibár* with the Jeunesse Musicale orchestra on an international tour. "Technology is amazing. My son is dead, but here he is alive playing beautiful music for us. Who knows, someday, maybe with technology, there will be no more death." Alice has no memory of a single exchange of abrasive words between the two of them. With Rafi's recording of Bohuslav Martinů's Second Cello Sonata playing in the background, Alice, with her eyes closed, says, "The only time that my son gave me pain was when he died."

THIRTEEN

First Flight

Alice still fondly remembers her first automobile ride with her adventurous father. He was one of the earliest in Prague to buy a car and to use it for his business. By the time Alice married, cars were still rare luxury items in Czechoslovakia; her nephew Chaim Adler recalls riding as a young boy with his uncle Leopold, Alice's new husband. Leopold sometimes let him steer on nearby country roads when they were searching for ideal spots to pick mushrooms or picnic.

Alice's inaugural flight was in 1959 or 1960, when she traveled on a four-engine Air France propeller plane from Tel Aviv to Paris to visit her son at the Paris Conservatory. In speaking of her first airborne adventure, Alice recalls the magic that by now has become so ordinary for many of us: the way the plane rose like a bird into the air, the way it soared smoothly, and the thrill she felt sitting among the floating clouds—even the excitement of turbulence. For Alice air travel meant the possibility of visiting corners of the earth she had known only from books. As air travel was shrinking the distances between continents, Alice hoped that the idea of all humanity belonging to one family was becoming a reality. "Maybe someday we will be smart enough to live together in peace," she says.

Although televisions were introduced in Czechoslovakia in 1948, Alice had no opportunity to see one there. Her initial exposure to television was in 1966, when it became available in Israel. And, almost childlike, she continues to marvel at the technology that we take for granted—that she can watch people from the past as if they are alive, or see something happening in the present in China or New York as she sits in front of her set in London.

Of all Alice's firsts, however, the first time she chose to leave her homeland for Israel was the most adventurous and, in some ways, the most courageous. The country suited Alice's personality in spite of its challenges. With her socialist leanings, her idealism, and her rejection of material values, Israel was an ideal new home. Her independence was respected by Israeli men and women, who worked together as equals in politics and war to bring their nation into being. Religion, nationality, and cultural tolerance were built into the fabric of their democracy. As Chaim Adler remarked, "It was far easier to be a secular Jew in Israel than in New York or in any European city." And many of the recent immigrants were European refugees like Alice.

Alice also found that the Israelis understood her. They revered their artists, great and small; they had built their country on intellect and music. In gratitude, Alice vowed that she would use all of her experience and knowledge as a musician and teacher to help expand, protect, and share the culture of her tradition with future generations.

On May 14, 1948, while Alice was still in Prague, Israel declared its independence in a dignified, moving ceremony in Tel Aviv. About two hundred invited guests gathered at 4:00 P.M. in the flower-decked Tel Aviv Art Museum on Rothschild Boulevard. A large portrait of Theodor Herzl hung behind a table with thirteen chairs arranged for members of the provisional government. The Palestine Philharmonic Orchestra, seated in the balcony, played the new national anthem, "Hatikvah" (The Hope), which was based on the same folk melody as Smetana's "Moldau." One by one each member of the new government signed the Proclamation of Independence, and in closing Prime Minister David Ben-Gurion rapped his gavel. "The State of Israel is established. This meeting is ended."

In her autobiography Golda Meir wrote of being unable to stop crying throughout the ceremony. "The State of Israel! ... and I, Golda Mabovitch Meyerson, had lived to see the day." As Ben-Gurion read the words explaining the reason for the new country—"The State of Israel will be open to Jewish immigration and the ingathering of exiles"— she sobbed aloud, thinking of all the lives that could have been saved and of those who were missing from the ceremony.

Half a century earlier, six years before Alice was born, at the first Zionist Conference, in Basel, Switzerland, Theodor Herzl, a Viennese journalist, had noted in his diary: "At Basel, I founded the Jewish state. If I were to say this today, I would be greeted with laughter." Confident in his belief, he wrote, "In five years perhaps, and certainly in fifty, everyone will see it." Herzl's work for a Jewish homeland had roots in his covering the trial of Captain Alfred Dreyfus, an officer in the French military, an innocent man who was convicted of treason and sentenced to death because of French anti-Semitism. After twelve bitter years of the Nazis' decimation of Europe's Jews and a fight for Israel's independence in a war against the British, Herzl's prediction had, at last, come true, though he was not alive to witness it.

By the time Alice and Rafi arrived at the Port of Haifa, the State of Israel was celebrating its first birthday. What struck her first were the exciting contrasts of Jerusalem: the beauty of the ancient city, with its camels and donkey carts, and the sights and sounds of twentieth-century life, from restaurants and nightlife to the noxious fumes created by cars and trucks. Most meaningful were the sounds of Beethoven and Mozart floating onto the streets from the windows of schools and apartments.

Alice still remembers the first time she heard ten-year-old Daniel Barenboim, who would become a world-famous conductor, play all of Mozart's sonatas for piano in the small concert hall of the music academy soon after he had immigrated from Argentina with his parents. Alice feels privileged to have known him as a child and beams when she talks about him: "Very unusual . . . absolutely genius." She is quick to remind that, even after so many decades, Danny took the time to visit her in London early in 2002, after he learned of Rafi's death. "He was best friends with my son. We talked about peace. He is an idealist." Barenboim and his late friend Edward Said, the Columbia University professor and writer, founded the West-Eastern Divan Orchestra, made up of both Israeli and Palestinian musicians as well as performers from other Arab countries. According to Barenboim, he conceived the orchestra as a project against ignorance. He said, "It is absolutely essential for people to get to know the other, to understand what the other thinks and feels, without necessarily agreeing with it."

Barenboim in accord with Alice believes that the Palestinians and Israelis can live together, and that making music together is one path to peace. With little money for rent in the early years, Alice shared the kitchen and bathroom of her and Rafi's apartment in Jerusalem with an Arab family. When she was working in the evenings or on weekends, they fed and watched over her son. Making friends of "enemies" has been one of Alice's keenest commitments. She is hopeful for the new peace efforts. "We must find a way to stop the killing," she says.

When Alice arrived in Israel, she was past her forty-sixth birthday and was unknown as a concert artist there. According to the critics of the day, including Max Brod, who heard her play with orchestras in Europe before the war as well as afterward in Israel, she was a great artist. She was a sensitive pianist who produced a warm, beautiful tone and performed with exquisite emotional rhythm. With her obedience to the composer's directions, Alice's playing was said to be reminiscent of the traditions of Dame Myra Hess and Mieczysław Horszowski. "I am a very simple person. And I play simply, without exaggeration," she says. Still in her prime, she might have been invited to perform with the Israel Philharmonic, which would most likely have led to international recognition. In fact, several of her fellow prisoners in Theresienstadt went on to successful careers after the war. Following his appointment as conductor of the Czech Philharmonic, Karel Ančerl led the Toronto Symphony, while Karel Berman, with his rich bass voice, enjoyed a major career in Eastern Europe, performing with both the Czech Philharmonic and the Prague Opera.

But careers in music are usually forged by ambitious performers during their youth. Alice was a true artist in that she continued to practice for five or six hours a day and polish her repertoire whether or not she had a paid concert. As she says, "I worked for my inner critic. I never cared what others thought." Chaim Adler thinks that if Alice had stayed behind the Iron Curtain in Prague, she would have continued to play with the Czech Philharmonic and probably would have been invited to tour throughout the Eastern Bloc countries. "Alice was certainly one of Czechoslovakia's finest pianists," her nephew says. All it would have taken for her to have been discovered and promoted by an international manager, her friends think, would have been an article or two about her past for American or British papers and successful recitals in New York and London. But Alice had no interest in exploiting tragedy for personal gain; most people who heard her play never knew that she was a refugee from a concentration camp.

Life and expectations had changed for Alice when she arrived in Israel. In solitude she could ask herself why such awful tragedy had struck not just her family but the Jewish people. And then she would marvel at the miracle of Israel and the hope it offered to the refugees. The Czech poet Rainer Maria Rilke had tried to explain that wisdom does not presume—wisdom is not knowing the elusive answers but fearlessly facing the questions. "Be patient toward all that is unsolved in your heart and try to love the *questions themselves* like locked rooms and like books that are written in a very foreign tongue." He went on, "Perhaps you will then gradually, without noticing it, live along some distant day into the answer."

Alice's embracing of the questions—her curiosity and openness to new and different experiences—is largely responsible for her inner peace and contagious, youthful happiness. Since her fearless first flights, Alice has never stopped observing, questioning, or learning from what each day brings—beyond books and degrees. That, for her, is the highest form of education.

FOURTEEN

Alice the Teacher

"I didn't want anyone to pity me," Alice says. "From my first day at the music academy, I kept silent about my past. I wanted no special privileges because I was a refugee. No one knew that I had survived a concentration camp. My students and their families did not need to be burdened with that part of my past."

Alice was no ordinary piano teacher. She threw herself into her work at the Academy in Jerusalem with the same enthusiasm, tolerance, gusto, and love with which she did everything else in her life. She recalls, "It was so thrilling because I had the new challenge of teaching advanced students to play a pianist's most difficult repertoire—not like giving lessons to beginners in Prague. I had to learn how to teach all levels of students who spoke many different languages." Alice was known as a tough but fair taskmaster. She held everyone to the highest standard. But students have said that they learned nearly as much from her eternal smile as they did from her words. Even when the nuances of the Hebrew language confounded her, her students could easily grasp Alice's emotional meaning.

Some students from Arab families came to her for lessons, and Alice warmly remembers one of them in particular, Killes. Now a teacher herself, Killes visited Alice in London four years ago and brought her student notebooks from fifty years earlier; she wanted to show her former teacher that she had written down every word, every instruction Alice had given during the lessons. She told Alice, "I wanted you to know that your way is the way I teach today. When I have a difficulty with a student, I review what you said. In this way, Alice, you are still my teacher."

Alice would not let Killes leave without playing for her. Killes felt a bit flustered. Then she looked into Alice's encouraging eyes and decided to try one of the last works she had studied with Alice before her graduation from the academy, Debussy's translucent "L'Isle Joyeuse." Afterward, Alice told her, "I am so proud of you." Killes says, "Her words sent me into the clouds."

Her former student Lea Nieman, when asked about Alice, comes back with "I can still smell those apples. She was so busy that she had no time to eat. Alice always kept apples in her bag—so fresh they still had green leaves attached—and when she was hungry she would eat one in the middle of the lesson. When she opened the door of her studio for me, the entire cozy room was scented with the odor of newly plucked fruit. After my lesson ended she would ask if I was hungry as she thrust an apple into my hand and sent me on my way. She was the kind of surrogate mother that music students love."

"Alice is a phenomenon," Nurit Vashkal Linder pronounces animatedly. "She was so energetic and generous. And she simply could not let you leave her studio without giving you something, a piece of music, a candy, a pencil. But more importantly, when you had difficulty learning a passage, she was remarkably patient. If Alice had a clock, it was invisible. My lesson lasted as long as necessary. When I had prepared particularly well, my lesson was longer. She was, and is, my most unforgettable teacher. I use my knowledge of music in everything I do and in everyday life."

Nurit makes special trips to London to visit Alice. "And she still insists on giving something to me before I leave," she says. "The last time I saw her, it happened that we had spent the entire morning together, and when the doorbell rang it was already one. It was Alice's daily delivery from meals on wheels. I grabbed my bag to leave, but Alice insisted that I stay for lunch, and proceeded to take out two plates and two forks and began to divide the meal—a bit of some kind of meat hidden under gravy, about two tablespoons of mashed potatoes, and maybe seven string beans. Not even enough for one normal appetite. But Alice was so insistent that I poured two small glasses of water and we sat together. And then Alice took a bite, and she declared, 'Marvelous.' It took me a whole moment to realize that she was referring to our dining together rather than to the food."

Nurit calls Alice every week from Israel. "I try to be helpful and Alice loves to speak Hebrew," Nurit reports. "She was a very strict teacher, despite her patience. Her standards were immensely high. I always felt sorry to disappoint her. She tried so hard with me."

As a teacher Alice draws her inspiration from the great composers; though they are of another, distant time, she has spent decades and continues to spend time exploring their thoughts and motivations. "My parents instilled in us a moral education by example," she says. She likes to point to Beethoven, who in spite of having little to call his own did his best to help where help was needed. Even though Beethoven could barely pay his own hotel bill, he once organized a benefit concert at the Grand Hotel Pupp in Carlsbad, Czechoslovakia, for an unknown composer who had fallen on hard times.

Alice speaks about Beethoven constantly; she admires his genius. "As I grow older, I appreciate Beethoven's depth more and more," she says. He created new music dictated by his fearless talent, breaking the bonds of established rules when necessary. Beethoven was the first musician to call himself an artist and to live by his work, beholden to no one. He searched for meaning in life, and he kept a notebook of philosophical quotations for inspiration. His understanding of human emotions was expressed through his timeless music. Alice likes to point out that Beethoven was free from conventional prejudice. He stood up to kings and princes when he disagreed with them, and Alice says, "He would not have been afraid to stand up to Hitler." While Beethoven's manners and his dress could be crude, his moral code—his unwavering stance for justice and freedom—was unimpeachable. "In the camp, I sometimes felt that I was protesting against the inhumanity of the Nazis when I played Beethoven," she says. "I could feel the audience breathing, feeling with me as they clung to their memories of a better time."

Alice also drew lessons, for her students and herself, from Schubert, Brahms, and Schumann, for their personal humility, respect for the talent of others, and the power of their works. When Beethoven died, Schubert, who was only thirty years old, said, "I still hope to make something of myself, but how can anyone do anything after Beethoven?"

Brahms left school when he was fifteen. Needing to earn his living, he had no opportunity to attend a university. But throughout his life he read philosophy, and, infinitely curious, he kept up with the latest scientific inventions. And he never forgot his humble beginnings or anyone who helped him along the way. Constantly Brahms reminded himself and others that the great poet Goethe had taught, "We only think we are original because we know nothing."

Robert Schumann also lived a generous life. Rather than promote his own career, he recommended other composers' works to publishers, and as a critic he called international attention to young, unknown musicians through lavish, though deserved, praise in his articles for *Neue Zeitschrift für Musik* (New Journal for Music). Schumann was responsible for discovering masterpieces of Schubert and Bach, who were largely forgotten after their deaths, and for arranging posthumous publications of their work.

As Alice raised her students on the music of Bach, she also made them aware of the artist's calling. No pupil escaped Alice's tutelage without knowing Bach's personal dictum: I compose for the glory of God and the entertainment of the soul. "Bach is the philosopher of music," Alice emphasizes as she puts her hands on her heart. "His music is like a puzzle. It takes many twists and turns, sometimes obvious but often elusive as it always goes forward just like our lives. For me he is the God of all of the Gods of Music."

To this day, at the age of 108, Alice begins her daily practice with a work by Bach from memory. She finds beauty and meaning in trying to solve the challenges her favorite composer offers up on the page. Relearning Bach's two- and three-part inventions from memory with uncooperative arthritic index fingers, she manages the difficult music with only four fingers on each hand. As Bach was the first pianist to play with his thumbs, using all five fingers, Alice laughs and says that she has progressed backward.

Throughout her many years, she has gleaned personal inspiration from the lives of these immortal composers, which she then poured into her performances. And she passed on her deep reverence to her students. If a student failed to know the first name of a composer whose work she was performing, Alice would admonish, "What? You don't know the name of your friend?" At the same time Alice was unaware of the love she stirred in the hearts of those budding pianists. Nor did she know that her influence would last a lifetime and beyond. Meira Shaham, the mother of the celebrated American Israeli violinist Gil Shaham, was one of those students.

MEIRA DISKIN SHAHAM

"Of course I would recognize her. She was my teacher." With tears welling in her eyes, Meira points to a recent photograph of Alice. "There she is. That's her. That's her smile." Meira, now a grandmother, had not seen or heard about Alice since she immigrated to the United States nearly forty years earlier. Meira wept too when she learned that Alice is a Holocaust survivor. "All these years I did not know. We students had no idea. She was so happy, always smiling, even when she was disappointed with our playing."

Meira studied piano with Alice throughout her high school years. As a budding scientist she went on to Hebrew University, where she earned advanced degrees in genetics. "She made me want to practice," Meira recalls. "Although I had taken my earliest lessons twice weekly with another teacher, I could get by without working between lessons. And anyway I had no piano at home. Practice was a foreign concept. But after I began to study with Alice, she got me to love to practice. At first I did it for her, in a neighbor's house after school. Then my friends and I started spending all of our weekends at the conservatory practicing for hours, just for the love of it.

"I did not become a professional, but I did give birth to the next generation and helped them to find their way along music's path. Yes, I was able to give something of what Alice had given to me to my children—her great, great love of music and musicians. So all her hard work was not lost." All of Meira's three children are musicians. Orli, her daughter, is a well-known concert pianist. Her oldest child, Shai, is a distinguished scientist specializing in developmental molecular genetics, although music is his lifetime avocation and he is a remarkable pianist. And Gil, Meira's middle child, is an internationally famous violinist.

And while Meira does her high-tech work in genetics, she is deeply involved in music through her children and friends. In whatever spare time she finds, she avidly attends concerts. "I represent the other half of the story—that is, the audience for music," she says. On New Year's Eve, 2010, Meira attended a joyous family concert in St. Louis. Orli's husband, David Robertson, the music director of the St. Louis Symphony, conducted the concert; Orli and Shai both played piano pieces; and Gil played Mendelssohn's Violin Concerto with the orchestra. St. Louis music lovers were fortunate to witness the tradition inherited and treasured from generation to generation.

EDNA ZAITSCHEK MOR

"I was in the middle of a session with a patient, an older woman," the Israeli psychoanalyst Edna Mor says, "when she mentioned, 'I listened to my mother play duets with Alice Herz-Sommer.' " Ignoring for a moment the rigid tenets of her profession, Edna says she told the woman that she also knew Alice. When she was young, she had taken piano lessons from her. Edna goes on to explain that, within that moment of mutual recognition, the patient's trust greatly increased. "And I believe that I was able to help her."

Edna talks about the first time she reconnected with Alice in London. "After nearly fifty years, Alice actually recalled a piece she said I had played very well. It was Chopin's Scherzo no. 2 in B Minor. And she reminded me that my boyfriend, Gideon [who later became Edna's husband], had learned Beethoven's Sonata, opus 2, no. 1, with her." Gideon worked with their teacher for only a year or two when he was a university student, and although he went on to become a biochemist, according to Edna, he has never stopped playing.

Edna studied with Alice for more than ten years. She was a talented pianist—but she is quick to confess that she was not one of Alice's star pupils. She was a shy girl who never wanted to be the center of attention. She felt that she could not face the competitive atmosphere of the conservatory and the requirements of public performances. "I never wanted to play in public, and still today I practice and play only for myself," she says.

Nevertheless Alice taught her as if she were pursuing a professional career. Edna became a private student and took her lessons in Alice's apartment so that she did not need to face the dreaded jury examinations by the academy's piano faculty. She remembers how the tiny front room in the apartment was completely dominated by the piano: "There was barely room to move about." Later Alice, with the help of her brother-in-law Dr. Emil Adler, was able to buy a larger place with a living room that could comfortably accommodate both of her pianos and guests for concerts.

Like Alice, Edna's parents were from Czechoslovakia, only they had escaped the Nazis to build new lives in Palestine in 1934. Both were amateur musicians and part of the genteel, music-loving world that was prewar Czechoslovakia. Edna's mother, a pianist, and her violinst father met Alice in Jerusalem. They too had lost many close relatives, including Edna's grandfather, in the Holocaust. The Nazis had arrested him in early 1940 for selling cigarettes on the black market in the streets of Brno as he struggled to support his family. After the war Edna learned that her grandfather had been murdered in Auschwitz.

Edna was Alice's only student to have even a vague idea of Alice's past, from overhearing her parents' conversations. But she never spoke about it with Alice as Edna understood that the subject was off-limits.

After Alice and Rafi moved into their larger apartment, Alice began to revive her prewar tradition of giving *Hauskonzerte,* and Edna's parents attended regularly. Most times Alice would serve tea and one of her luscious Czech cakes. The discussions were always lively, and then the topic would invariably turn to local politics. After an hour or so Alice would go to the piano, where she would play a formal program for another hour or two. In this way Alice and a few of her émigré friends re-created warm moments of their familiar life in Czechoslovakia, the way it was before.

ESTER MARON KRIEGER

Before she left for London to visit Alice in the fall of 2010, Ester practiced Chopin's Ballade in G Minor countless hours daily for nearly two months. Although Ester had not seen Alice in more than forty years and had performed the Ballade in concert countless times, she was nervous as she prepared to play it for her former teacher. Alice was thrilled with Ester's performance. "Magnificent. Your playing never stops growing," she told her. Ester felt the same surge of hope that she'd felt half a century earlier when Alice approved of her playing.

Like Alice, regardless of the impediments life has thrown her way, Ester has enthusiastically made the best of her situations through music. When in 1962 the time came for her to do her obligatory two years of military service, she was worried about time for practicing and being away from music. Never at a loss for ideas, she asked if she might be permitted to teach music during her army years. Without the usual teacher training courses, she was sent to teach in two schools in Israel's most northern city, Kiryat Shmona, very close to the Syrian and Lebanese borders. It was an area that, at the time, was considered too dangerous for civilian teachers. Ester paid a visit to Zadik Nahamu Yona, the principal of Tel Hai, one of the schools, on a sultry day before the opening day of school to get his instructions and advice.

The principal explained that Ester would be teaching the youngest children: third through eighth grade. Most of her students would be French-speaking children of immigrants from Morocco, Tunisia, and Algeria. The principal, the soldiers, and the teachers were mostly Jewish immigrants from Europe and the Middle East. Admitting that she had not been trained in music education, Ester asked to see the textbooks and an outline of the curriculum. "I am sorry that we do not have many books. We do own a few recorders, drums, and cymbals. You are free to use them," the principal told her. He paused before saying, "I love music. These poor children need this in their lives. Please—do your best, but know that you are on your own." Later Ester would learn that this compassionate, intelligent, down-to-earth man, an immigrant from Iraq, had no college degrees. Yet he ran a superb school, evoking the best from his soldier-teachers and a deep love of learning in the children.

Ester thought of Alice and how she made music sing wherever she was. "Teaching is love and a teacher must love to teach"—Alice's words rang strongly in Ester's memory. During her two years in Kiryat Shmona, Ester produced concerts and even fully staged and costumed musicals with her students. "This was the best training I could have had— far better than a graduate school laboratory," she claims. "I think that teaching is always a matter of improvising, adjusting to get the most of each individual." And that, according to Ester, describes the way Alice was with her students. "She was very modest and patient as she encouraged me to try ever more difficult pieces."

Ester began lessons at the Academy with Alice when she was sixteen. Four years later and only two months before her graduation examination, the doctors put Ester's right wrist in a cast to correct a previous injury. She was panicked because she was unable to practice, but Alice comforted her, saying, "Don't worry, you will be fine. We will have at least a month after your cast is off to prepare. I will give you a lesson every day."

"And she kept her word, every day we worked, until I was finally ready for my graduation program. May I say that I received the top marks?"

Ester was admitted on full scholarship to the New England Convervatory of Music, only to learn that she could not major in accompanying because it was not offered in the degree program. With Alice-like perseverance, she persuaded the president of the school to design the program she wanted. He did, and Ester received their first degree in vocal accompanying. Thanks to her, the program continues to flourish.

Ester's only child, a daughter, Michal, was raised in the distant shadow of Alice's influence and is now a cellist in the Haifa Symphony. Describing their visit to Alice in September 2010, Michal said that Alice asked her why she had chosen the cello. "I always knew that I wanted to be a musician just like my mother. I heard my mother accompanying a cellist and loved the sound," Michal answered. "Alice asked me if I played the Dvořák concerto, and she started singing the theme." Michal told Alice that of course she had learned it in school, but she had not had a chance to play it with an orchestra. "Well, what are you waiting for?" Alice quipped before adding, "You must work and work again on the slow movement. With this piece you will learn to master the performance with an orchestra weaving your part in and out—as if you were in a conversation about love, never saying goodbye, always returning. It is all warmth and love, never angry or aggressive. Your tone must be a laser beam to the heart." Then suddenly dropping that conversation, Alice asked if Michal played concerts with Ester.

"Of course," Michal answered. "I love playing with my mother."

Alice continued, "It was my great joy to play concerts with my son. Nothing, nothing made me happier. I think he liked it too. I know the cello repertoire by heart. Your mother, Ester, is an excellent pianist. Ex-cel-lent," Alice repeated, emphasizing each syllable. In parting Alice added, "We are so lucky. We are the richest people in the world. Much richer than millionaires. People who don't know music are very, very poor!"

Ester's most recent hurdle is facing mandatory retirement from her work at the Levinsky Teachers College. Actually she has already retired twice, and each time was called back because she is so specialized that she cannot easily be replaced. In May 2011, Ester presented what was supposed to be her farewell concert with her current students. But, as for Alice, retirement for Ester is highly unlikely. She has already increased her practice hours in preparation for other options.

Asked what is the most important lesson piano teachers can share with their students, Alice says, "Love to work." She mentions that, when Bach was asked how he managed to write so much great music, he answered, "Hard work . . . anyone who works as hard as I do will be successful." Alice continues, "And this is true for all teachers of all subjects. . . . Instill a love of work, a love of practicing or of cleaning the kitchen until it shines. Love to make things better. Love the process of learning. We must learn to enjoy work because it is good in and of itself and not because of the triumph we hope to achieve."

"Love to work" has been Alice's lifelong guiding principle, which she also imparted to her students, teaching them to try to perfect even one short phrase by practicing the passage hundreds or thousands of times until it is fluent.

"When I start a new piece," Alice explains, "it takes time, and little by little, sometimes after months, when I know it like my nose, I can call it my own." Alice insists that she practiced all kinds of exercises to free her technique. "This is, I believe, the secret to my sight reading. My eyes see groups of notes that my fingers obey because of the scales and practicing all sorts of patterns.

"When you truly love your work, you are much happier. And I can say that your chance of success is greater." Not only did Alice teach her piano students to love to practice but her code extended beyond music. "Enjoy even menial tasks," she says. "They help to overcome life's greater challenges."

Alice throws her head back in hearty laughter when she finds a new solution to a difficult passage that she has practiced for at least one hundred years.

INTERLUDE

The Lady in Number Six

The tree-lined street in London's Belsize section is quiet. Robin Tomlinson, the affable directing manager of the apartment house, is taking in the morning air with his short-haired dog when a passerby asks him where the music is coming from.

"Aw yes. She lives on the first floor. She plays the piano all day," Robin says in his warm Irish accent.

The other tenants recognize their effervescent oldest neighbor as Alice the pianist. They set their clocks by her practice schedule. And they look forward to a jovial exchange whenever they run into her in the hallway. Although they know that she plays from memory, they are always surprised and flattered to find that her memory is just as sharp when it comes to the names of their children, grandchildren, and pets. Alice discusses the latest international political news, and whenever something happens in the world, "What does Alice think?" becomes a common question among the tenants. They know that she always has an opinion. Even frequent guests to the building know that a lady called Alice lives there.

Robin enjoys promoting the best interests of his tenants. "Running a building full of amazing people is about much more than making money. I look at my tenants as my family. I am responsible for them and for their homes. It is my job to keep them happy. If they are happy, I can enjoy my sleep," he says.

Robin and his wife occupy the top floor of the five-story building, where they tend the flowers in their sprawling roof garden and welcome visits from the residents. Until recently Alice was a frequent guest, always eager to enjoy the ever-changing landscape of the garden and sit, if the day was sunny, in the warm and healing light. Sometimes she would arrive to watch the hummingbirds at work. Teasing Alice, Robin would tell her, "Those tiny birds are putting on a special show to thank you for your music." Alice would take the time at sunset, when the scents of flowers on windless nights are strongest, to remember similar moments, standing on her Jerusalem balcony and surveying the ancient landscape. On the London rooftop the aroma of the jasmine, lilies, and roses was tangible. Alice particularly loved the red roses climbing on the fence. Robin sometimes plucked a few for her to take home for the top of her piano. Alice no longer visits the garden. Climbing the stairs is too taxing.

Most of the tenants marvel at Alice's playing. They are astonished by her continued dedication to her art. Once, when Alice was hospitalized after a small accident, Robin visited her and threatened to send her piano to the hospital if she did not come home soon. "Send it today," she quipped. "I need to practice." According to Alice's friend and neighbor Valerie Reuben, the only time the music stopped was when Alice's son died. "We feared for her life because the music had gone silent." After several weeks the tenants rejoiced when they once again heard Alice's piano. She began slowly, playing for only a few minutes before she would close the cover on the piano. But when she regained enough strength to begin the day playing Bach preludes and fugues, one by one the neighbors thanked her for the music. They did not speak of the death, but Alice understood the meaning of their words.

Many years after Alice moved in, a new tenant surprised Robin when she knocked at his door early one morning to thrust a paper in his hand. "Please sign this," she said, "for the sake of the sanity of everyone who lives here. This terrible piano playing night and day must stop."

Robin invited her in and suggested that they talk in his garden. He read the typed page as they climbed the stairs to the roof. Once outside, Robin directed the woman to a chair. "Do sit down," he ordered. A tall, well-built man, he towered over her as he remained standing. The paper the new tenant wanted him to sign and distribute to all the tenants was a petition to forbid Alice to practice.

Furious, he took a slow, deep breath before speaking. "This is outrageous," he began. He tore the paper in half as he spoke. "Do you know who Alice is? Have you no heart? Under no circumstances will I curtail her piano playing. Telling her that she cannot play in her own apartment would be tantamount to murder. No," he said, his voice rising. "I will never circulate this ugly petition you are so proud of. Our tenants love Alice and they love hearing her play. The entire neighborhood loves her playing."

Years later Alice learned of this incident. She has never stopped thanking Robin, whom she considers her "very good friend." And when asked how she likes her apartment house, Alice responds, "Extraordinary." She repeats the word. "Wonderful people live in this building. I am very lucky."

Among the first questions Alice asks the pianists from New York City she meets are these: "How are your neighbors? Can you practice at home?"

FIFTEEN

Circle of Friends

"I have always made friends easily," Alice says. "When you love people, they love you too."

"My friend," an endearment that Alice never uses lightly, is possibly the most supreme compliment a Czech of the twentieth century can pay to anyone. During the Nazi and Communist periods, friendships were tested and could have meant the difference between prison and freedom, or even between life and death. Friendship implies not only mutual understanding and mutual ideals but also unspoken trust. Alice knows the value of close human contact; she has forged deep connections through the bonds of shared memory. Her warmth and smile and inquisitive mind welcome others—people gather around her as if attracted by a magnet—while the joy she feels at being alive is contagious to those closest to her.

Alice inspires the gift of friendship.

ANITA LASKER-WALLFISCH

Peter Wallfisch, a pianist and professor at the Royal Academy of Music, began visiting Alice after she settled in London. Peter had escaped from Germany to Palestine before the war and had many friends and endless topics of conversation in common with Alice. His wife, cellist and author Anita Lasker-Wallfisch, was a founding member of the English Chamber Orchestra.

Anita arrived in London in 1946, after the British army liberated Bergen-Belsen. She had lost her parents in the camps and would later write a memoir called *Inherit the Truth* about her parents' attempts to escape Germany and her own experiences in Auschwitz.

Music was Alice and Anita's most obvious bond, but the deeper understanding between them developed from their common backgrounds. Both Anita and her husband were from Breslau, a city known for its love of music. Alice herself was no stranger to Breslau, as she had received great acclaim for the several concerts she had played in this medieval city in the eastern corner of Germany. As it did in Alice's family, music reigned in the Lasker household. Anita's mother, Edith, was a beautiful violinist, and all three of her children took music lessons. One of Anita's sisters, Marianne, managed to reach England shortly before the outbreak of the war, but her sister Renata was arrested by the Gestapo and deported to Auschwitz together with Anita.

And much as the Herzes did, the Laskers would hold chamber music evenings nearly every week, as well as afternoon literary discussions over coffee and cake on Saturdays. Despite the fear and deprivation during their last months together before deportation, Anita's father, Dr. Alfons Lasker, read *Don Carlos* aloud to his family and had begun Goethe's *Faust.* In a letter addressed to Marianne in London in 1941 Anita's mother wrote, "We never knew how marvelous everything was then!!! Well, perhaps, in spite of everything, we will all five of us sit down at a cozy round table again one day!"

When Anita speaks of the war, she says, "The cello saved my life. Literally." She goes on to explain, "When prisoners first arrived in Auschwitz, they were immediately treated to a kind of initiation ceremony where their heads were shaved and their arms were tattooed with identification numbers. This work was done by female prisoners. I was expecting to go to the gas chambers, as that was Auschwitz. Then one of the prisoners asked me, 'What do you do for work?' The answer that fell out of my mouth, 'I play the cello,' was completely ridiculous. I had just turned seventeen, and I had no occupation other than student. That prisoner whispered, 'Thank God, you will be saved.' " The Auschwitz-Birkenau women's orchestra needed a cellist.

Anita was taken to audition for the orchestra's conductor, Alma Rosé, a well-known violinist from Vienna and a niece of Gustav Mahler. Although Anita had not played or even seen an instrument for more than a year, she was accepted as the orchestra's only cellist. The all-girls ensemble was in no way a traditional symphonic orchestra. Rosé arranged music to accommodate the available instruments—violins, recorders, mandolins, guitars, accordions, a double-bass, a flute, and a cello—and the various abilities of the players. She rehearsed "her girls" with uncompromising discipline, trying to make each performance a musical experience. They would play at the gates of the camp as the masses of prisoners were marched off to work in the early morning, and again at nightfall as the prisoners were marched back inside the walls. They would play the marches in rain and snow, and they would play waltzes and incidental pieces for Nazi events. "Just as the Nazis liked things, orderly and neat," Anita says.

One day, after Anita had been in the orchestra for some time, the infamous Nazi physician Josef Mengele entered their barrack and asked to hear Schumann's "Träumerei." Anita sat down with her cello and played the piece.

When typhus ran rampant in Auschwitz, Anita contracted the disease and was held in the so-called sick bay or infirmary. She was nearly delirious from high fever when she heard the Gestapo pointing out patients who were to receive immediate "special treatment"—the gas chamber. As soldiers were preparing to cart her off, she heard an officer yell, "No, not that one, she is the cellist." In that moment Anita recognized that she still had an identity even though her name had been replaced with a number.

In London, Anita was occupied with her orchestra and her growing family of distinguished musicians. Her grandson Benjamin Wallfisch is a noted conductor and composer, and her son, who bears the same name as Alice's only child, Raphaël, is an internationally known cellist. Alice would often visit Anita and keep her company when she was babysitting one of her young grandchildren. The two women would discuss music and memory often over coffee and cake in Anita's garden. Alice particularly loved those afternoons during the early summer when gentle breezes brushed the little white blossoms of Anita's mock orange bushes. After Rafi's death, Anita began a habit of driving across London on Saturday afternoons to spend a few hours with her friend. They did not talk much and rarely mentioned the past but would play Scrabble in English together. Alice looks forward to Saturdays with Anita.

GENEVIÈVE TEULIÈRES-SOMMER

Alice says effusively, "Geneviève is the best daughter-in-law in the world." And for extra emphasis she adds, "Extraordinary!" Returning the compliment, Geneviève says, "But you are the best mother-in-law." Friends agree that both must be true. More than ten years after Rafi's death, Geneviève remains completely devoted to Alice. She has played a large role in protecting her mother-in-law's independence. When anyone asks about Alice's preferences, Geneviève usually answers very respectfully, "Why don't you ask Alice?"

In spite of her daily practice schedule and the responsibilities of teaching cello at the École Normale de Musique in Paris all week, Geneviève travels regularly to London for the weekend to spend time with Alice. She then teaches on Saturdays as well, at London's Guildhall Junior School of Music. And whenever other commitments—running the summer music festival in Gex that she founded with her husband or serving on examination juries at the conservatory—keep her away from Alice, she stays in constant touch by phone. When in London, Geneviève often drives her own part-time housekeeper to Alice's flat to do a thorough cleaning, for which Alice is grateful.

WENDY

At ninety-one years old Wendy, eccentric English Wendy—no one seems to know her last name—is known for her good heart. And no one knows whether she was ever married, divorced, or widowed, or if she is wealthy or struggling. In conversation she gives the impression of being a creation of her own imagination; in practice, however, Wendy is a caregiver and, at times, a lifesaver. Large-boned and tall, with long dark hair sprinkled with strands of white, she travels around the London neighborhoods on her bicycle in all kinds of weather. And she writes poems that she delivers aloud on birthdays to those who have the patience to listen.

Wendy had been browsing in neighborhood bookstores for years and, like so many others, was curious about the source of the music emanating from the window of Alice's building when she passed at the same time each morning. She began conducting her own investigation, asking everyone who emerged from the building if they knew the pianist. She learned that the music came from a European woman of a certain age, and one morning she waited for the music to stop. When a small lady appeared outside the front door, Wendy asked, "Are you, by chance, Mrs. Sommer?" True to her generous spirit, Alice invited Wendy to visit that afternoon for tea. Since that first meeting Wendy has come by nearly every day—often, like a doctor making rounds, stopping in for just five minutes to see if Alice needs anything. One day in early July, for example, Wendy just showed up— or "pitched up," as the English say—at Alice's apartment, wearing a long bright-colored flowing skirt with a strapless orange cotton top. She was making one of her several daily visits to check on her elderly friends, and Alice had the five o'clock slot. Alice introduced her to the other guests who happened to be visiting as "Wendy the poet" and incited her to recite from memory one of her lengthy verses.

Several years back, when Alice was only 104, she fell when she was out for one of her long walks and was hospitalized for a few weeks because of the bruises. The day she returned to her apartment, Wendy paid her late afternoon visit and was astonished to find Alice alone; she felt strongly that Alice should not be left by herself at night after her ordeal. With little floor space in Alice's one-room flat, Wendy slept in a chair at her friend's side—that night, and every night over the following two weeks.

During the early fall of 2010, only a few weeks before Alice's 107th birthday, Wendy made her usual stop to find Alice lying on the floor unable to move. Wendy flew into action, alerting the paramedics, who rushed Alice to a hospital. She had had a mini-stroke and was treated and released a few days later. Since then Wendy has increased her visits to twice daily. Yet Wendy as a person remains a mystery; Alice has no idea where Wendy lives, and she does not have her telephone number.

EDITH STEINER-KRAUS

As much of an enigma as Wendy is to Alice, Edith Steiner-Kraus is the opposite. Alice has known Edith for more than seventy years. Not only did Alice know Edith in Prague before the war but they also survived Theresienstadt together and both immigrated to Israel. Alice exchanges regular telephone calls with Edith, who still lives in Israel. They never forget to call on each other's birthday. And it is through Edith that Alice keeps up with Israeli politics and the prospects for peace.

Born in Vienna to Czech parents, Edith is ten years younger than Alice. When she was six her family moved back to Karlovy Vary, known as Carlsbad, a small city in Bohemia famous for its spa. Shortly after beginning piano lessons, Edith was recognized as a child prodigy and invited to perform for celebrities. Alma Mahler happened to hear her and was so enchanted with the girl that she recommended her to her friend the pianist Artur Schnabel. At first suspicious of one so young, Schnabel, after listening to her audition, accepted her as the youngest student in his Berlin master class.

Like Alice, Edith was forging an outstanding career in Prague and the surrounding area when the war began. Alice still remembers the first time she heard the pretty, slim woman play Smetana's dances. "She was a great pianist," Alice says admiringly. When she and her husband were deported to Theresienstadt, Edith continued to practice her piano one hour per day and to perform as much as she could. Viktor Ullmann persuaded Edith to play the premiere of his Sixth Piano Sonata, composed in Theresienstadt. Later in Israel, where she also concertized, Edith became recognized as an Ullmann expert, frequently performing all of his eight sonatas.

Edith immigrated to Palestine with her second husband and baby girl in 1946. After working in a tie factory, she was eventually given an appointment as a professor of piano in the Music Academy of Tel Aviv. She was well settled and able to help when Alice arrived, in 1949. Together again, they continued their personal and musical friendship. Before Alice left Israel for England, however, Edith suffered a stroke that left her unable to play. For some time she continued to lecture even though her sight was failing. Today she is nearly blind.

Their deep, unbroken connection to music continues to be life-sustaining for these two women. And they both understand the importance of solitude. For them, solitude is not lonely. It is the quiet that is essential for listening. In solitude we call up from the depths of our souls those insights and memories that are beyond the visible or the verbal. It is in the stillness of solitude that an artist may become most creative. As artists, Alice and Edith have recognized that the world can be a lonely place. But when there is someone—even one person—who shares our background, our perspective, thoughts, and feelings, that loneliness is shattered. For Alice one of those rare persons is Edith.

VALERIE REUBEN

"The English don't ask questions," Alice observes. "They are very polite, but they don't ask questions. Everyone said that Valerie was British. She speaks perfect English." But one day Alice asked her where she was born. Valerie explained that her ancestors were from Romania and Poland, but that she and her parents had escaped Hitler's grasp because they were all born in England.

A slim, elegantly dressed and coiffed woman of indeterminate age, Valerie Reuben, a leading member of the tenants' committee of their apartment building, has watched over Alice and helped her in myriad ways since Alice moved to London. Valerie made an enormous difference in Alice's routine when she introduced her to the University of the Third Age. They would travel together to classes and continue their discussions at home.

"I have never known anyone like Alice," says Valerie. "She has such a strong character and always pulls through. I try to help her but find that I get much more just by being in her remarkable presence." Valerie adds that Alice surprises her sometimes with a touch of mischievous humor. "Once when I told her I was packing for my holiday she came to my flat to see what I would be wearing and commented on all the items I was taking.

"Now that she is well past one hundred, I do worry about

her and look in more often than before. It is not just a pleasure but a privilege to know her."

Alice describes Zdenka Fantlova as "my very good Sunday friend. She comes every Sunday and stays with me all afternoon." A youngster of only ninety years, Zdenka looks like a beautiful middle-aged Czech woman. She finds all possible shortcuts through the maze of London's narrow, winding streets to drive from her apartment facing Hyde Park to Alice's home in Hampstead every week.

Zdenka is Alice's closest Czech friend in London. Born in a midsize city some distance from Prague, Zdenka too is a survivor. Only through luck, youth, and good health did she manage to survive first Theresienstadt, then Auschwitz, Gross Rosen Mauthausen, and Bergen-Belsen. She later wrote a memoir about her life under the Nazis called *The Tin Ring*.

In Theresienstadt, Zdenka heard Alice play all of the Chopin études at a concert. She remembers being transported out of time and place by the music. "For the duration of the concert I could imagine that life was normal and that we would soon go home again to our familiar life. It meant much to me, but as I was a teenager I did not dare to approach Frau Sommer," Zdenka recalls.

"After the war, when I was recuperating in Sweden, I noticed in the paper that Alice was going to play a concert in Stockholm. Nothing could stop me from going to that concert. Alice opened with Beethoven's *Appassionata* Sonata. Once again I was mesmerized by her playing and longed to meet her." Although Zdenka waited for a while after the concert in a crowd of well-wishers, she was ultimately too shy to greet the pianist. Forty years would pass—Zdenka became a well-known actress in Australia, married, and had a daughter—before she would meet Alice face-to-face in the 1980s.

Zdenka and her husband decided to make London their home, moving into a spacious apartment in the city's West End. She had missed Europe and wanted to be closer to pieces of her past. At the same time, she had spent so many years in an English-speaking country that it seemed more comfortable to live in Britain, within a short flight or overnight train trip to the Continent. She finally met Alice through a mutual Czech friend who took her to visit one afternoon soon after Alice arrived in London. Alice played a Chopin waltz for her that day. Zdenka was enraptured with the music and the memories.

Alice would later give Zdenka piano lessons. Until she was nearly one hundred, Alice would make the trek to Zdenka's apartment every week by subway, even though Zdenka tried to provide her with transportation. Alice always refused, saying that she preferred the excitement of the underground. And Alice would teach Zdenka with the same care and demand the same high standards as she had with her most professional students. The lessons always ended the Czech way, with coffee and little cakes and poppy-seed strudel. Sometimes, especially in summer, when wild berries were in season, Zdenka would prepare Alice's much loved *palačinke,* tiny, wafer-thin pancakes topped with wild strawberries and whipped cream. As they discussed books they were reading or Alice tried to interest Zdenka in her philosophy classes, they were reminded of the days of their youth.

After Rafi died Zdenka's piano lessons stopped and the coffee meetings were moved to Alice's apartment. Still, each Sunday, Zdenka spends most of the day with her friend. She brings familiar homemade Czech delicacies, and Alice prepares the tea. Alice relishes those hours spent speaking the Czech of her childhood and catching up on the news. While they do not talk of the war years, Alice loves to hear stories about Zdenka's father, Arnošt Fantl, and to read his notebooks, which glimmer with practical wisdom. Alice agrees with most of his thoughts. But her favorite words are, "Never try to have too much of anything in life, just what you need and a little more. When you die, all you will take with you is what you have given to other people." A businessman by profession, he was never too busy to engage with his growing children over dinner every evening at seven. For Alice, Zdenka is a reminder of what she used to call home.

Although Alice no longer ventures outside, she exercises by walking with her friends in the lobby of the building. She never complains. As she learned long ago, "Complaining does not help. It just makes everyone feel bad." It's no surprise that friends take their leave from her feeling refreshed and often uplifted.

Anita, Geneviève, Wendy, Edith, Valerie, and Zdenka have become Alice's surrogate family and caretakers— extending themselves as needed, watching over her, helping her to continue the independent life she knows and loves. And they do not leave empty-handed. Each of the women says over and over how much Alice has given back to her—each has been inspired, each touched in her own way by a fresh dose of Alice's "yes" to life.

Thankful for her friends, Alice is acutely aware that human contact in all its many forms does indeed keep you human.

CODA

Alice Today

"The life of one that laboureth and is contented shall be made sweet."
—*Ecclesiastes*

For the last two or three years Alice had ended her phone calls with me, "Come soon to London," and a touch of her Czech humor: "You never know if I will be here." On Thanksgiving 2010, I scrambled to put the obligatory turkey and potatoes into the oven for our annual celebratory dinner before leaving for the airport. It was the first time in my life that I had abandoned my daughter on our favorite holiday. Family and friends arrived as I finished packing. With an admonition to remember to baste the bird, I ran out the door barely in time to catch the afternoon flight. It was scheduled to arrive at 6:15 the next morning, November 26, Alice's 107th birthday.

On the morning of her birthday, Alice awoke early to brilliant fall sunlight. The London sky was a shimmering clarity
of blue, unusual at that time of year. It reminded her of the
light in Kafka's steel-blue eyes and his ways of understanding
how to find the bright side of everything. At 8:30 she began
her day earlier than usual, practicing a Bach invention. An
hour later she had to stop to attend to preparations for guests
who were certain to arrive. No celebration had been planned,
no invitations had been issued, and no cake had been ordered, but Alice knew that countless friends, acquaintances,
strangers, and family members would be dropping by. As
she had nothing else to serve, she arranged on platters all of
the chocolates from two boxes that she had received as early
birthday gifts. After placing one dish at a time on the tray
table in front of her chair, Alice wrapped a colorful scarf
around her shoulders and fastened a single strand of small
ivory beads around her neck. She unlocked the door to her
apartment and propped it open in anticipation.

One of the first to arrive was her elder grandson, David,
whose smile matched the mood of the day. David needed to
rush off to his office, but Alice was clearly thrilled to see him
even for a few minutes. They blew kisses to one another
across the room. Alice's friend Sonia Lovett, with permission from Alice, had discreetly set up a camera to record the

special day and brought birthday wishes from her father. A cellist in the famous Amadeus Quartet, Sonia's father first got to know Alice in London, but his father—also a cellist— had been a close friend of Alice's in Israel.

By 10:00 A.M., Zdenka had swept in on the arm of a younger man with the longest-stemmed red roses Alice had ever seen, and with blossoms so large that at first Alice thought Zdenka had brought paper flowers. She could not stop talking about them and wanted to know where they were grown. She was also interested in learning more about Zdenka's friend Tomas Schrecker, who was visiting from Australia. He had been a child on one of the Winton Kinder-transports in 1938 that took Jewish children from Prague to live with foster families in England.

One by one Alice's friends and acquaintances continued to pour into her tiny apartment. As Zdenka said a hurried goodbye, Christopher Nupen, a film director, and his wife arrived with two young pianists, both foreign students at the Royal Academy. The small room was now overflowing. Conversation was constantly interrupted by the many telephone calls from well-wishers around the world. "Hello," Alice would answer in English. Then, with her face breaking into a smile as she recognized the voice, Alice would continue in the language of the caller. The morning ended with the students performing duets on Alice's somewhat out-of-tune piano. In spite of all the attention, Alice said farewell to her visitors so she could quietly eat her lunch, delivered, as usual, from meals on wheels, and then rest.

The afternoon saw another round of guests. Geneviève arrived from Paris, and soon after, Anita stopped by, bringing a present of warm slippers that Alice could step into without bending over, the way she had done with difficulty to tie her sneakers. Talk was intimate and quiet, mostly about music. When it turned to the difficulty of explaining to today's youth the feeling so many had for great music a half century earlier, Alice was quick to remind them of something Kafka had written: "Our art consists of being dazzled by the Truth." But Kafka did not really know anything about music, the group agreed. "Yes," Alice countered, smiling, "but he understood our respect for the music. How often Kafka said, 'Writing is a kind of prayer.' Listening to music, playing concerts, even practicing is a kind of prayer."

The large decorated chocolate cake Sonia managed to find in a nearby bakery was Alice's favorite, and after successfully blowing out her many candles, Alice ate the first piece. Later in the afternoon Alice greeted another crowd: an elderly couple, survivors, accompanied by their children, who wanted to honor Alice; a composer friend; and Alice's neighbor Valerie Reuben. As the room was crowded, several people waited patiently outside in the hall for a chance to speak to Alice. Jacqueline Danson had driven more than one hundred kilometers from her home in Hampshire to bring her mother, Ruth, to see Alice. Later Jackie would comment that Alice's "unsullied sweetness" was as heartening as ever. Since her earliest childhood, Ruth Boronow Danson has known and loved Alice. Like Anita, she had grown up in Breslau, where her mother, Kaethe, was a piano teacher. Ruth's father, the late Dr. Ernst Boronow, a well-known dentist and intellectual, sponsored Alice's concerts there. Through his profound love of music Ernst became one of Alice's closest friends. Arrested on Kristallnacht, he was imprisoned in Buchenwald for a short time and released. Dr. Boronow lost no time fleeing to England in March 1939 with his family. Alice reconnected with Ernst and his children when she visited London in the 1960s.

Ruth clearly remembers being taken to Alice's Breslau concert in 1927. Jackie said that when her "Opa" (grandfather) was listening to Alice practice or even to a phonograph recording or radio broadcast, "entering the room felt like walking into a synagogue or church."

At a quarter after four, the Czech ambassador to Britain, Michael Žantovský, arrived with his wife and an enormous, elegant arrangement of pink and white flowers. The ambassador tried to make a formal presentation, but Alice repeatedly interrupted him. In a decidedly Alice moment, full of mischief and humor, she said that she was more interested in understanding how genes work than in getting awards. Žantovský then tried using musical terms to describe how two genes might accidentally meet, intertwine, and finally end their game by becoming one entirely new melody, and he began his speech anew: "As the permanent representative of the Czech Republic, I have come today on behalf of my government to—" only to be interrupted again by Alice, who was unsatisfied with his layman's explanation. "Doesn't anyone in this room understand genes? I know that when my husband and I made a baby, that child inherited our musical talents through our genes. But how? I want to know how genes work and why they sometimes don't work."

"Alice," Ambassador Žantovský said, stroking the back of her hand, "please let me make my presentation, and I promise that I will bring a great Czech geneticist to visit you who can answer all of your questions. Now can I present the award?" Incorrigible, Alice looked at the ambassador and asked, "Who made you do this?" Always the consummate diplomat, he answered, "Alice, this award is a gift to you from my government. Now please do not interrupt, let me make my presentation so that I will not lose my job." Both of them laughed, and Alice finally allowed the ambassador to deliver his brief speech before the small group of friends standing in the little room.

The award was the Czech Ministry of Culture's 2010 Artis Bohemiae Amicis medal for promotion of Czech culture abroad. In his speech Ambassador Žantovský mentioned that his grandmother had also been a prisoner in

Theresienstadt and that just maybe she had heard Alice's concerts in the camp. He also explained that before being posted to London he had served as the Czech ambassador to Israel. At last he opened the box containing an impressive brass plaque engraved with a citation to Alice.

Once again the candles were lit and everyone sang "Happy Birthday" in a cacophony of Czech, Hebrew, German, and English. Alice was beginning to tire from the day's excitement.

The experience of the Holocaust has affected each survivor and family differently. Elie Wiesel has spent his life thinking about the total madness he witnessed day in, day out, the evil that destroyed his family and millions of the Jewish people. He has argued with God and concluded, "God is the silence of God." Alice agrees with Wiesel, and with Einstein, who said that he believed in "Spinoza's God who reveals himself in the orderly harmony of what exists, not in a God who concerns himself with the fates and actions of human beings." Alice talks of the end of her life and the realization that she, as well as all of us, is a minuscule particle in the infinity of God or what we call the universe. Alice is confident when she says, "I have lived in music, I will die in music," which is her mortal way of connecting to infinity.

Alice is able to leave the past behind; she draws her strength from living in the present. After the Velvet Revolution of 1989, when the Communist government of Czecho-slovakia was overthrown and Václav Havel became the country's first free president, unrestricted travel became possible there. The former prisoners of Theresienstadt began to organize and hold memorial ceremonies in the camp. Year after year, hundreds of survivors would gather for reunions in Theresienstadt; performances of *Brundibár* and Verdi's Requiem were reconstructed in the old horse stadium. Alice has never attended. She has never wanted to return to the country of her birth. The Czechs have yet to restore her citizenship. Her passport reflects her Israeli citizenship, and she holds permanent residency in Great Britain. This is Alice's present.

Still, the award from the Czech ministry has meaning for her and elicits beautiful memories of "the way it was." How proud her mother would have been of the government's formal recognition of her daughter.

Alice came into my life at a time when I needed her inspiration and was most open to learning from her. My vision was not what it used to be. The brightest day looked hazy. And then I bumped into an accidental miracle, or at least the event had a miraculous effect on me. I was making a documentary about Alice, who at the time was only 103. We had spent the majority of the afternoon filming, and later in a restaurant I could not find my glasses to read the menu. Assuming they had fallen off my head in Alice's tiny apartment,

I asked a young assistant, Sean, to retrieve them. Returning empty-handed, Sean reported that the glasses were nowhere to be found and that I must have lost them elsewhere.

Alice was waiting at the door when I arrived to interview her the next day. Smiling broadly, she said, "I found your glasses this morning." As she handed them to me, she mentioned that she had also found one of the lenses, which had fallen out.

I could hardly believe that Alice's ancient eyes were far more acute than mine or even Sean's. I realized then that this was not about just a pair of glasses and the ability to see well or even to see at all.

Alice's vision has enabled me to face the greatest test of my life, the illness of my only child. It was a shock that has forced me to face the limits of existence and to find strength and calmness in Alice's example. Her ability to accept reality, not to allow anger or frustration to dominate even a few moments of her time, to garner the courage to trust her own instincts rather than depend on the approval of others, and to hold fast to hope continue to work inside me. And yes, there is Alice's laughter, effervescent laughter every day. Long before modern-day explorations of the healing possibilities of laughter, Alice understood the immense health benefits that laughing induces, how when we laugh the body takes in more oxygen. Her laughter is a blessing that has made me, and so many others, feel better; her influence has led me to a more peaceful life, clearer vision, and contentment and gratitude for life itself.

The morning after the birthday celebration when I stop in, Alice is standing in front of her windowsill, which is lined with a few small plants—gifts from strangers. As she gazes outward, she catches glimpses of the late fall colors and the eternally green ivy, bits of the natural world that are so much a part of her. "Look, how beautiful. Nature," she tells me. Quoting her own translation of Spinoza, Alice says, "We are nature. God is nature." She pauses to reflect. "Impossible to believe, I am one hundred and seven years old. You know that I am very independent and have the freedom to think for myself. I am so happy that I woke up today."

◄○►

As I write this, Alice Herz-Sommer has just celebrated her 108th birthday. She continues to practice and polish her repertoire with miraculous concentration, always searching for that elusive perfection. One of her visitors recently asked her why she still spends so much time practicing the same pieces. Folding her arms, she looked him straight in the face. "I am an artist. Some days I admire myself. Not bad, I think. But the longer I work, the more I learn that I am only a beginner. No matter how well I know a work of Beethoven, for example, I can always go deeper, and then deeper still. One of the rewards of being a musician is that it is possible to practice the same piece of music and discover new meaning without boredom for at least a hundred years. I study the language of music with the same fervor that scholars reexamine the holy scriptures. The artist's job is never done. It is the same with life. We can only strive towards rightness. As with music, I search for meaning. I practice life."

Stefan Zweig marveled that, during the first half of the twentieth century, man realized the impossible of yesterday: conquest of the air, radio transmission of the human word, the splitting of the atom, the curing of the most hideous diseases. He wrote, "Not until our time has mankind as a whole behaved so infernally, and never before has it accomplished so much that is godlike." Zweig continued, "Our greatest debt of gratitude is to those who in these inhuman times confirm the human in us." As a witness to the twentieth century, Alice has lived through the extraordinary cultural and scientific accomplishments Zweig chronicled; she experienced the highest rewards civilization has to offer—the power of music, literature, art, technological innovation, science, and philosophy to bring out the best in our humanity—and she survived the greatest degradation of the human spirit the Western world has known. And yet, in immersing herself in art while remaining closely connected to the world around her, to her music, and to what Kafka called that something "indestructible" deep within her being, Alice has found lasting happiness—which for all of us may be the ultimate source of eternal youth.

IN ALICE'S WORDS

I am so old because I use my brain constantly. The brain is the body's best medicine.

Only when we are old do we realize the beauty of life.

Gratitude is essential for happiness.

A sense of humor keeps us balanced in all circumstances, even death.

Complaining does not help. It only makes everyone feel bad.

Laughter is wonderful. It makes you and everyone else feel happy.

Love to work. When you love your work you are never bored. Boredom is unhealthy.

When we love our work, we can enjoy a sense of achievement, every small achievement.

Generosity above all.

School is important, but what children learn in the atmosphere of their homes lasts for life. The beautiful, intellectual, and musical atmosphere of my childhood has sustained me until today.

School is only the beginning. We can learn all our lives.

I grew up with friendship. I fell in love with my future husband's mind and his knowledge. In marriage, friendship is more important than romantic love.

I am never tired because my mind is active.

Stay informed. Technology is wonderful.

I learned to move forward with hope.

Children need unconditional love to grow and develop into full human beings. My advice is to reason with your children, never use harsh words. Patience, kindness, and love—this is the food a child needs.

Be kind. Kindness is free. It costs you nothing, and the rewards are great for everyone.

When I play Bach, I am in the sky.

My world is music. Music is a dream. It takes you to paradise.

I am richer than the world's richest people, because I am a musician.

Children must study music. It helps with everything in life. This beauty is always in my mind.

When I am with young people, I am the youngest.

I love people. I am interested in the lives of others.

No one can rob your mind. I admire the Jewish people because of their extraordinary commitment to high education. Education of the children is a most important family value.

Understanding of others can lead to peace.

I can say war only leads to war. Nearly every religion in the world says "Thou shalt not kill," yet most religions kill in the name of God. Even Hitler's daggers said *"Gott mit uns."*

Every day is a miracle. No matter how bad my circumstances, I have the freedom to choose my attitude to life, even to find joy. Evil is not new. It is up to us how we deal with both good and bad. No one can take this power away from us.

Life is beautiful. Sitting together and talking about everything with friends is beautiful.

We do not need things. Friends are precious.

We need to treasure time. Every moment that passes is gone forever.

Music saved my life. Music is God.

My optimism has helped me through my darkest days. It helps me now.

The more I read, think, and speak with people, the more I realize just how happy I am.

When I die I can have a good feeling. I have done my best. I believe I lived my life the right way.

ACKNOWLEDGMENTS

Above all I am deeply indebted to Alice Herz-Sommer. It is my hope to have captured her life justly and pass along if only a modicum of the courage and inspiration that she has given me.

An extraordinary debt of gratitude is owed to my friends Marion Wiesel, who suggested writing this book; Elie Wiesel and President Václav Havel, for their generous contributions; and Oldřich Černý, executive director of Forum 2000 and Prague Securities Institute, who discovered and translated previously neglected material on the life of Michal Mareš. And I am grateful to Dr. Willard Gaylin for his lifelong intellectual sustenance and courage.

Warmest thanks to Alice's friends, former students, and relatives in London, New York, and Israel who graciously let me interview them, cheerfully taking my calls over the past six years; their information and insights have been invaluable.

My profound thanks to Lukáš Přibyl, historian and documentary film director, who researched the Terezin archives for relevant information; to the late Joža Karas, who generously shared his research on Alice's life based on his taped interviews with her in Israel in the 1970s; to Milan Kuna, the Czech musicologist; to the late Karel Berman and Paul Sanford for their hours of sensitive conversations and wealth of accurate memories; to Polly Hancock for her sensitive photography; to Sophia Rosoff for her depth of understanding; to Dr. Arnold Cooper for his support; to the late Dr. Viktor Frankl and Hans Morgenthau for sharing their memories; to Eva Haller for her endless encouragement and enthusiasm; to Carsten Schmidt, the biographer of Felix Weltsch, who found and translated a letter written by Leopold Sommer in the archives of Hebrew University of Jerusalem; to Yuri Dojc for his beautiful photographs; to Laura Siegel for her brilliant help; and to Chaim Adler, Martin Anderson, Dr. Sigrid Bauschinger, Ralph Blumenau, Clemente D'Alessio, Jacqueline Danson, Ruth Boronow Danson, Yuri Dojc, Lucinda Groves, Zdenka Fantlova, Katya Krasova, Anita Lasker-Wallfisch, Annie Lazar, Hilde Limondjian, Nurit Linder, Anthony LoPresti, David Lowenherz, Ester Maron, Keith Menton, Edna Mor, Lea Nieman, Valerie Reuben, Lawrence Schiller, Meira Shaham, Dr. Alan Skolnikoff, Connie

Steensma, Geneviève Teulières-Sommer, Robin Tomlinson, Ela Weissberger, and Ambassador Michael Žantovský for their invaluable contributions.

This book would not be complete without a very special note of infinite gratitude to my agent and friend Marly Rusoff for her faith and support; to Cindy Spiegel, my publisher and editor, for her belief in the project and her brilliant edits; and to Lorna Owen, for her understanding and constant encouragement. And to my beloved daughter, Anna Elizabeth Stoessinger, to whom I dedicate this book.

NOTES

PRELUDE

xiv "Where they burn books": Heinrich Heine, *Almansor: A Tragedy* (1823), trans. Graham Ward (True Religion, 2003), p. 142.

xiv Raphaël, or "Rafi": Alice named her son Bedřich Štěpán Sommer and called him Štěpán. When she and her eleven-year-old son immigrated to Israel, they changed his name to Raphaël. Throughout the book I refer to him as "Raphaël" or "Rafi," as Alice does today. Even in recounting stories of him as a baby, she always refers to him as Rafi and never as Štěpán.

xvii "This is our answer to violence": Leonard Bernstein, *Findings* (New York: Simon & Schuster, 1982), p. 218.

xix "He is a wise man": Epictetus, quoted in Lloyd Albert Johnson, *A Toolbox for Humanity: More Than 9000 Years of Thought* (Trafford Publishing, 2006), p. 158.

I. ALICE AND FRANZ KAFKA

6 **"Someone must have slandered Josef"**: Franz Kafka, *The Trial*, trans. Breon Mitchel (New York: Schocken Books, 1998), p. 3.

6 **"When Gregor Samsa woke up one morning"**: Franz Kafka, *The Metamorphosis*, trans. Stanley Corngold (New York: W. W. Norton, 1996), p. 3.

6 **"It was late evening when K. arrived"**: Franz Kafka, *The Castle*, trans. Mark Harman (New York: Schocken Books, 1998), p. 1.

6 **"I am familiar with indecision"**: Ronald Hayman, *Kafka: A Biography* (Oxford University Press, 1982).

7 **"It had never been my intention"**: Max Brod, *Franz Kafka: A Biography*, trans. G. Humphreys Roberts and Richard Winston (New York: Da Capo Press, 1995), p. 249. This statement was the last paragraph in Kafka's brief résumé:

RÉSUMÉ

I was born in Prague on July 3, 1882, attended the Altstadter elementary school to the fourth class, then entered the Altstadter German State Gymnasium. At the age of eighteen I began my studies at the German Karl Ferdinand University [Charles University] in Prague. After passing the final state examination, I entered the office of Attorney-at-Law Richard Lowy, Altstadter Ring, on April 1, 1906, in the capacity of probationer. In June I took the oral examination in history and in the same month was graduated with the degree of Doctor of Laws.

As had previously been agreed with the attorney, I had entered his office only in order to acquire a year's experience. It had never been my intention to remain in the legal profession.

On October 1, 1906, I entered his service and remained there until October 1, 1907.

Dr. Franz Kafka

7 **"I could not understand"**: Ibid., p. 26.

8 **"That was what he was like"**: Ibid., p.107.

9 **"To have one person"**: Ibid, p. 196. The entire quote is, "There is no one here who wholly understands me. To have one person with this understanding, a woman for example, that would be to have a foothold on every side, it would mean to have God."

10 **"Such gentle hands"**: Ibid., p. 196.

10 **"That was the beginning"**: Ibid., p. 196.

2. A TOLERANT HEART

20 **"Peace with honor"**: Neville Chamberlain, speech at Heston Aerodrome and 10 Downing Street, September 30, 1938, in James Cushman Davis, *The Human Story: Our History, from the Stone Age to Today* (New York: HarperCollins, 2003), p. 326.

22 **"the Jews of Bohemia and Moravia"**: Dr. Detler Muhlberger, *A Brief History of the Ghetto of Terezin* (Oxford, 1988). http://www.johngoto.org.uk/terezin/history.html. Ronald H. Isaas and Kerry M. Olitzky, *Critical Documents of Jewish History: A Sourcebook* (Northvale, N.J.: Jason Aronson, Inc.), 38–48.

3. PEELING POTATOES

30 **"It's no accident many accuse me"**: Interview with Oriana Fallaci published in *Ms.,* April 1973, p. 76.

36 **"Although I don't know much about music"**: Menahem Meir, *My Mother Golda Meir* (New York: Arbor House Publishing Company, 1983), p. 46.

37 **"It is the duty of everyone"**: Howard Taubman, *The Maestro: The Life of Arturo Toscanini* (New York: Simon & Schuster, 1951), p. 224.

37 **"doing this for humanity"**: Ibid., p. 227.

38 **"The fact that Toscanini and other"**: Menahem Meir, *My Mother Golda Meir* (New York: Arbor House Publishing Company, 1988), p. 46.

39 **"Nearly religious devotion"**: Ibid., p. 45.

5. STARTING OVER

55 **"You can't go home again"**: *You Can't Go Home Again* is the title of a novel by Thomas Clayton Wolfe (1900–1938), an American from North Carolina. The book was published posthumously in 1940 by Harper and Brothers. Ending that book, Wolfe wrote, "You can't go back home to your family, back home to your childhood . . . fame . . . back home to a young man's dreams of glory and to places in the country, back home to the old forms and systems of things which once seemed everlasting but which are changing all the time—back home to the escapes of Time and Memory."

Wolfe's books were bestsellers in Germany, where he was lionized by literary society and was especially friendly with Mildred Harnack, who with her German husband, Arvid, organized a resistance group with their anti-Nazi friends and former university students. The Nazis gave the group a code name, Die Rote Kapelle (The Red Orchestra). In 1936 Wolfe made his last trip to Berlin, to attend the Olympics. During that visit he witnessed brutal incidents against Jews. Inspired by Mrs. Harnack, he wrote a short novella, "I Have a Thing to Tell You," about his experiences, which was published in *The New Republic*. After the story appeared in three installments on March 10, 17, and 24, 1937, the Nazis banned Wolfe's books and prohibited him from traveling there. Arvid Harnack was arrested and executed in December 1942. On orders from Hitler, Mildred, an American from Wisconsin, was beheaded in Plotzensee Prison in early 1943.

62 **"A group of Revolutionary Guards and other gangs"**: Michal Mareš, *Dnešek* 1, Prague, July 11, 1946.

62 **"If there is real freedom"**: Michael Mareš, *Přicházím z periferie republiky (I Come from the Periphery of the Republic)*, trans. Oldřich Černý (Prague, Academia Press, 2009).

66 **He confirmed his plan:** According to Pavel Koukal, the editor of Mareš's autobiography, *Přicházím z periferie republiky*, Mareš "would in the future like to live alongside Alice Herz Sommer, whose son Štěpán [Rafi] he wanted to adopt." On page 177, Koukal references a letter to Mareš from Ivan Bambas-Bor from August 21, 1947. Bambas-Bor invites Mareš to Kutná Hora, a town forty kilometers from Prague, to deliver a lecture. Expecting Mareš to travel with Alice, he also invites Alice to play a concert following the lecture.

6. THE TIN SPOON

69 **"Music is love, and love is music"**: Melissa Muller and Reinhard Piechocki, *A Garden of Eden in Hell*, trans. Giles MacDonogh (London: Macmillan, 2006), p. 67.

72 **"Her death was not terrible for her"**: Ibid., p. 80.

76 **"We are all well except Štěpán"**: Leopold Sommer, trans. Carsten Schmidt, Letter to Willy and Felix Weltsch, Israel, Jerusalem Hebrew University (JNUL), Arc. Ms. 418 Felix Weltsch, February 26, 1940.

78 **"Love does not consist in gazing"**: Antoine de Saint-Exupéry, *Wind, Sand and Stars,* trans. Lewis Galantiere (New York: Harcourt, 1939), p. 73.

7. NEVER TOO OLD

84 **"is not actually a university in the normal"**: Ralph Blumenau, London, Amazon.com profile of Ralph Blumenau.

87 **"without music life would be"**: Friedrich Nietzsche, *Twilight of the Idols* (1895), trans. Walter Kaufmann and R. J. Hollingdale, Maxims and Arrows, Para 33.

8. MUSIC WAS OUR FOOD

97 **"You are no doubt speaking"**: Tim Smith, Baltimore *Sun,* October 2, 2010.

98 **sitting alone among many elderly:** Ivan Klíma, *The Spirit of Prague,* trans. Paul Wilson (New York: Granta Books, 1993), p. 22.

105 **"Chopin's Divine Mirror"**: *Music in Terezin 1941–1945* (Stuyvesant, N.Y.: Pendragon Press, 1990), pp. 172–73.

105 **She smiles recalling Pavel Haas's:** While Pavel Haas was writing songs based on Chinese poetry in a concentration camp, his actor brother, Hugo, was playing a leading role in a Hollywood film with Gregory Peck. Haas perished in Auschwitz. Hugo, who had

escaped to California before the war with his non-Jewish wife, lived out his days playing small character roles in numerous films.

10. SNAPSHOTS

122 **"Nothing misled the German intellectuals":** Stefan Zweig, *The World of Yesterday* (Lincoln: University of Nebraska Press, 1964), p. 362.

122 **"Then came the Reichstag fire":** Ibid., pp. 364–65.

125 **"Memory is the scribe":** Aristotle, quoted in John Bates, *A Cyclopedia of Illustrations of Moral and Religious Truths* (London: Elliot Stock, 1865), p. 583.

11. MAN IN THE GLASS BOOTH

132 **"was not, in any sense":** Golda Meir, *My Life* (New York: G. P. Putnam's Sons, 1975), p. 179.

132 **"If only the defendant":** Elie Wiesel, *All Rivers Run to the Sea: Memoirs,* trans. Marion Wiesel (New York: Schocken Books, 1995), p. 348.

134 **"I was just responsible":** The Trial of Adolf Eichmann, Record of Proceedings in the District Court of Jerusalem, Volume 5, Israel State Archives, 1995, p. 1982.

134 **"Yes, but he was Jewish":** Peter Z. Malkin and Harry Stein, *Eichmann in My Hands* (New York: Warner Books, 2000), p. 110.

135 **"a transmitter":** Adolf Eichmann Trial Transcript, *Great World Trials,* edited by Edward W. Knappman (Canton, Mich.: Visible Ink, 1997), pp. 132–337.

135 **"I could not take my eyes":** Wiesel, *All Rivers Run to the Sea,* p. 347.

135 **"I never did anything"**: Adolf Eichmann Trial Transcript, *Great World Trials,* edited by Edward W. Knappman (Canton, Mich.: Visible Ink, 1997), pp. 132–337.

135 **"Now that I look back"**: Roger Cohen, "Why? New Eichmann Notes Try to Explain," *The New York Times,* August 13, 1999. Cohen writes, "[Eichmann] complained regularly about death-camp quotas not being fulfilled, about the problems of getting all French Jews to the death camps, and about the intermittent failure of the Italians to cooperate. As late as 1944, he played a leading, and open, role in the killing of Hungarian Jews, and in August of that year he reported that four million Jews had died in the death camps and another two million at the hands of the Nazis' mobile extermination units in Eastern Europe. At no point did he show the least compunction over the planning, organization and execution of what became known as the Holocaust."

135 **"Legally not, but"**: Adolf Eichmann Trial Transcript, *Great World Trials,* edited by Edward W. Knappman (Canton, Mich.: Visible Ink, 1997), pp. 132–337.

136 **"I will leap into my grave"**: Ibid., pp. 132–337.

136 **"banality of evil"**: Hannah Arendt, *Eichmann in Jerusalem: A Report on the Banality of Evil* (New York: Penguin, 1977), p. 252.

136 **"The sad truth"**: Ibid., p. 276. "[Arendt] concluded that Eichmann's inability to speak coherently in court was connected with his incapacity to think, or to think from another person's point of view. His shallowness was by no means identical with stupidity. He personified neither hatred or madness nor an insatiable thirst for blood, but something far worse, the faceless nature of Nazi evil itself, within a closed system run by pathological gangsters, aimed at dismantling the human personality of its

victims. The Nazis had succeeded in turning the legal order on its head, making the wrong and the malevolent the foundation of a new 'righteousness.' In the Third Reich evil lost its distinctive characteristic by which most people had until then recognized it. The Nazis redefined it as a civil norm. Conventional goodness became a mere temptation which most Germans were fast learning to resist. Within this upside-down world Eichmann (perhaps like Pol Pot four decades later) seemed not to have been aware of having done evil. In matters of elementary morality, Arendt warned, what had been thought of as decent instincts were no longer to be taken for granted." From the Introduction by Amos Elon, p. xiii.

137 **"there is a strange interdependence":** Ibid., p. 288.

138 **"Wouldst thou know thyself":** Edgar Alfred Bowing, *Friedrich Schiller* (London: John W. Parker & Son), 1851.

139 **"I only said what everyone":** Max Bruch, Letter to Estera Henschel, Musikantiquariat Dr. Ulrich Drüner, Stuttgart, Catalogue 65, 2009, p. 23.

12. NO HARSH WORDS

145 **"We began a simple life":** Paul Tortelier and David Blum, *Paul Tortelier: A Self-Portrait* (London: William Heinemann, 1984), p. 112.

148 **"The art of Johann Sebastian Bach":** Ibid., p. 24.

13. FIRST FLIGHT

155 **"The State of Israel is established":** Golda Meir, *My Life* (New York: G. P. Putnam's Sons, 1975), p. 228.

155 "The State of Israel! . . . and I": Ibid., p. 226.

156 "The State of Israel will be open": Ibid., p. 227.

156 "At Basel, I founded": Ibid., p. 226.

156 "In five years": Ibid., p. 226.

157 "It is absolutely essential": Daniel Barenboim, http://www
     .west-eastern-divan.org/the-orchestra/daniel-barenboim.

159 "Be patient toward all": Rainer Maria Rilke, *Letters to a Young
     Poet,* trans. M. D. Herter (New York: W. W. Norton, 1934), p. 27.

14. ALICE THE TEACHER

166 "I compose for the glory": Joseph Machlis, *The Enjoyment of
     Music* (New York: W. W. Norton).

15. CIRCLE OF FRIENDS

193 Zdenka Fantlova, *The Tin Ring: How I Cheated Death,* trans.
     Deryck Viney (Newcastle upon Tyne, U.K.: Northumbria Press,
     2010), p. 35.

CODA: ALICE TODAY

200 "Our art consists of": Brod, *Franz Kafka.*

200 "writing is a kind of prayer": Ibid., p. 214.

203 "God is the silence": Elie Wiesel, *Ani Maamin,* trans. Marion
     Wiesel (New York: Random House, 1973), p. 87.

203 "Spinoza's God who reveals himself": Alberto A. Martinez,
     *Science Secrets: The Truth About Darwin's Finches, Einstein's
     Wife, and Other Myths* (Pittsburgh: University of Pittsburgh
     Press, 2011).

207 **"Not until our time"**: Zweig, *The World of Yesterday,* p. xxi.

207 **"Our greatest debt of gratitude"**: Ibid., p. xii.

207 **"indestructible"**: "Man cannot live without a lasting trust in something indestructible within himself." Brod, *Franz Kafka,* p. 214. According to Brod, "In this sentence Kafka formulated his religious position."

BIBLIOGRAPHY

Arendt, Hannah. *Eichmann in Jerusalem: A Report on the Banality of Evil.* New York: Penguin, 1977.

Bascomb, Neal. *Hunting Eichmann.* New York: Houghton Mifflin, 2009.

Bernstein, Leonard. *Findings.* New York: Simon & Schuster, 1982.

Brod, Max. *Franz Kafka: A Biography.* Translated by G. Humphreys Roberts and Richard Winston. New York: Da Capo Press, 1960.

Bryant, Chad. *Prague in Black: Nazi Rule and Czech Nationalism.* Cambridge, Mass.: Harvard University Press, 2007.

Elon, Amos. *The Pity of It All: A Portrait of the German-Jewish Epoch, 1742–1933.* New York: Henry Holt, 2009.

Fantlova, Zdenka. *The Tin Ring: How I Cheated Death.* Translated by Deryck Viney. Newcastle upon Tyne, U.K.: Northumbria Press, 2010.

Frankl, Viktor E. *Man's Search for Meaning.* Translated by Else Lasch, Harold Kushner and William J. Winslade. Boston: Beacon Press, 1959.

Garrett, Don, ed. *The Cambridge Companion to Spinoza.* New York: Cambridge University Press, 1996.

Gilbert, Martin. *A History of the Twentieth Century: Volume II: 1933–1951.* New York: William Morrow, 1999.

——. *The Holocaust: A History of the Jews of Europe During the Second World War.* New York: Holt, Rinehart and Winston, 1986.

——. *Israel: A History.* New York: William Morrow and Company, 1998.

——. *The Righteous: The Unsung Heroes of the Holocaust.* New York: Henry Holt, 2003.

Goldsmith, Martin. *The Inextinguishable Symphony: A True Story of Music and Love in Nazi Germany.* New York: John Wiley & Sons, 2000.

Goldstein, Rebecca. *Betraying Spinoza: The Renegade Jew Who Gave Us Modernity.* New York: Schocken Books, 2006.

Herzl, Theodor. *The Jewish State.* New York: Dover Publications, 1988.

Kafka, Franz. *The Castle.* New York: Schocken Books, 1998.

——. *Dearest Father.* Translated by Hannah and Richard Stokes. Surrey, U.K.: One World Classics, 2008.

——. *Diaries 1910–1923.* Translated by Joseph Kresh and Martin Greenberg, with the cooperation of Hannah Arendt. New York: Schocken Books, 1948.

——. *Letters to Friends, Family, and Editors.* Translated by Richard and Clara Winston. New York: Schocken Books, 1977.

——. *The Metamorphosis.* Translated by Stanley Corngold. New York: W. W. Norton & Company, 1972.

——. *The Trial.* Translated by Breon Mitchell. New York: Schocken Books, 1998.

Karas, Joža. *Music in Terezin, 1941–1945*. Stuyvesant, N.Y.: Pendragon Press, 1990.

Kennedy, John F. *Why England Slept*. Garden City, N.Y.: Dolphin Books, 1962.

Klima, Ivan. *The Spirit of Prague*. Translated by Paul Wilson. New York: Granta Books, 1974.

Kuna, Milan. *Hudba na hranici života (Music on the Edge of Life)*. Naše vojsko—Český svaz protifašistických bojovníků. Praha 1990.

Kurz, Evi. *The Kissinger Saga: Walter and Henry Kissinger, Two Brothers from Furth, Germany*. London: Weidenfeld & Nicolson, 2000.

Lang, Jochen von, editor. *Eichmann Interrogated: Transcripts from the Archives of the Israeli Police*. Translated by Ralph Manheim. New York: Farrar, Straus & Giroux, 1983.

Levi, Erik. *Music in the Third Reich*. London: Macmillan, 1994.

Levi, Primo. *Survival in Auschwitz*. Translated by Stuart Wolf. New York: Simon & Schuster, 1996.

Lipstadt, Deborah E. *The Eichmann Trial*. New York: Schocken Books, 2011.

Malkin, Peter Z., and Harry Stein. *Eichmann in My Hands*. New York: Warner Books, 1990.

Meir, Golda. *My Life*. New York: G. P. Putnam's Sons, 1975.

Meir, Menahem. *My Mother Golda Meir*. New York: Arbor House, 1983.

Miller, James. *Examined Lives: From Socrates to Nietzsche*. Farrar, Straus and Giroux, 2011.

Muller, Melissa, and Reinhard Picchocki. *A Garden of Eden in Hell*. Translated by Giles MacDonogh.

Newman, Richard, with Karen Kirtley. *Alma Rose: Vienna to Ausch-witz.* Portland, Ore.: Amadeus Press, 2000.

Rilke, Rainer Maria. *Letters to a Young Poet.* Translated by M. D. Herter. New York: W. W. Norton, 1954.

Robertson, Ritchie. *Kafka.* New York: Sterling, 2010.

Saint-Exupéry, Antoine de. *Wind, Sand and Stars.* Translated by Lewis Galantiere. New York: Harcourt, 1939.

Seckerson, Edward. *Mahler.* New York: Omnibus Press, 1983.

Taubman, Howard. *The Maestro: The Life of Arturo Toscanini.* New York: Simon & Schuster, 1951.

Tortelier, Paul, and David Blum. *Paul Tortelier: A Self-Portrait.* London: William Heinemann, 1984.

Wallfisch-Lasker, Anita. *Inherit the Truth: A Memoir of Survival and the Holocaust.* New York: St. Martin's Press, 2000.

Wiesel, Elie. *Ani Maamin: A Song Lost and Found Again.* Translated from the French by Marion Wiesel. New York: Random House, 1973.

———. *Memoirs: All Rivers Run to the Sea.* New York: Alfred A. Knopf, 1995.

Zweig, Stefan. *The World of Yesterday.* New York: Viking Press, 1943.

About the Author

CAROLINE STOESSINGER is a pianist who has appeared on the stages of Carnegie Hall, Lincoln Center, and the Metropolitan Museum of Art; in concert halls from Tokyo and Johannesburg to the Sydney Opera House; and from the White House to Prague Castle. For twenty-five years she has performed repeatedly with the Tokyo String Quartet, Shanghai Quartet, Talich Quartet, and the Brooklyn Philharmonic Orchestra. Lukas Foss composed Elegy for piano and orchestra for Stoessinger, who premiered the work in New York and Oslo with the composer conducting. She has produced and written the scripts for internationally televised programs and public events including the dedication of the Schindler violin at the United States Holocaust Memorial Museum in Washington, D.C., and the first New York production of *Brundibár*. She served as artistic director at the Cathedral Church of Saint John the Divine and the Legacy of Shoah Film Festivals in Prague and New York. A consultant to the Shelley and Donald Rubin Foundation, Stoessinger has spoken worldwide for the Young Presidents' Organization, World Business Council for Sustainable Development, and the Chief Executive Forum. She is artistic director of chamber music at the Tilles Center, professor and artist-in-residence at John Jay College, artistic director of the Newberry Chamber Players at the Newberry Opera House, and president of the Mozart Academy. She lives in New York City, where Mayor Bloomberg recently presented her with an American Dreamer Award.